cathedrals of the world

TRANSLATION: STUDIO TRADUZIONI VECCHIA, MILAN

© 2006 White Star s.p.a.
Via Candido Sassone, 22/24
13100 Vercelli, Italy
www.whitestar.it

TRANSLATION: STUDIO TRADUZIONI VECCHIA, MILAN

ISBN-13: 978-88-544-0178-5

REPRINTS:
 2 3 4 5 6   10 09 08 07

Printed in China
Color separation: Chiaroscuro, Turin

cathedrals of the world

text by Graziella Leyla Ciagà

WHITE STAR PUBLISHERS

TEXT

by GRAZIELLA LEYLA CIAGÀ

Editorial Director

VALERIA MANFERTO DE FABIANIS

Editorial Coordinator

FEDERICA ROMAGNOLI

Graphic Designer

CLARA ZANOTTI

5 ■ The interior of St. Peter's Basilica in Rome, with the bronze baldacchino which frames the papal altar.

7 ■ Detail of the scupted decorations at the sides of the main doors of Chartres Cathedral.

10-11 ■ The vaulted roof of St. Mark's Basilica, Venice.

12-13 ■ Inside view of the octagon of the crossing in Ely Cathedral, United Kingdom.

CONTENTS PAGE

Introduction

This book examines how the various types of "basilica" and "cathedral" have evolved. It covers the major historical turning points of church architecture, from its Early Christian, Romanesque and Gothic origins, through its evolution in the Renaissance and Baroque periods, right up to the latest contemporary architecture.

Thirty six buildings are included, built in twelve countries and three continents: Europe, Asia and America. The reader is thus provided with a broad overview of the different styles and characters that these buildings have taken on in different geographical and cultural contexts.

The book examines the history of these extraordinary monuments of Christianity. It describes them throughout their never-ending transformations, from the point of view of construction techniques, liturgical requirements, architectural language and decorative elements. These, then, were the aspects that were kept in mind when choosing from the vast number of basilicas and cathedrals all over the world. The focus was mainly on those buildings which, due to their exemplary value, set the standard not just in their own historical period, such as Hagia Sophia in Constantinople or Notre-Dame Cathedral in Paris, but also in the centuries that followed – as is the obvious case of St. Peter's Basilica in Rome. As for the 20th century, our aim was to provide a panorama of current trends in architecture for large religious complexes. The works of the most prominent contemporary architects were selected, taking into account not just the architectural debate, but also the significance that building a basilica or cathedral has today.

Furthermore, the selection was limited to churches with the title "basilica" or "cathedral," and those terms were interpreted strictly in their liturgical sense. Indeed, in canonical law, the title "basilica" denotes a church to which the Holy See has conferred a particular privilege, which depends on certain conditions. These could be the age, size or artistic or religious value of the church, or the richness of the holy relics that it houses. Meanwhile the title of "cathedral," which was introduced in the Middle Ages, refers to the main church of a diocese. That where the bishop's seat (*cathedra* in Latin) is located.

In Italian the cathedral is also known as a "duomo" or house of God. The only exception to this selection criterion was the sanctuary of San Padre Pio da Pietrelcina. This was included by virtue of the great interest generated by the architecture – designed by Renzo Piano using utterly innovative technical and spatial solutions. The choice was also influenced by the extraordinary popular devotion surrounding the charismatic figure of Padre Pio, who draws vast numbers of pilgrims to San Giovanni Rotondo from all over the world.

The sections on each basilica and cathedral include some standard information such as the approximate surface area, including any buildings annexed to the church (atriums, sacristies, chapels, memorial chapels, baptisteries, and so on), without taking into account underground spaces (crypts, lower churches, etc) or any monastic buildings. This way, the reader should be able to get an idea of the general size of these buildings, which are often very large; just think of St. Peter's in Rome, which covers a surface area of over 215,000 sq. ft (19,974 sq. m).

Half of the churches included are among the monuments on the UNESCO World Heritage List, either mentioned specifically or because they are situated on sites that have been declared of particular interest (such as, for example, the historic centers of Venice, Rome, Florence, Istanbul, Moscow or Mexico City). This large category includes the basilicas of Sant'Apollinare in Classe (Ravenna), St. Sophia (Istanbul), St. Mark (Venice), La Madeleine (Vézelay), St. Peter (Rome) and the Redentore (Venice), as well as the cathedrals of Pisa, Speyer, Durham, Paris, Chartres, Amiens, Canterbury, Burgos, Florence, Moscow (St. Basil), Mexico City and Brasília.

BASILICA OF

SANT'APOLLINARE IN CLASSE

[RAVENNA ■ ITALY]

The basilica of Sant'Apollinare in Classe lies on the rural plain 3 miles (5 km) south of Ravenna; in Roman times, the area was the location of the ancient Augustan harbor and a large town. The basilica was built by Bishop Ursicino, and consecrated by Emperor Maximian in 549; it is considered one of the most important buildings dating from the Byzantine exarchate. In fact, after the fall of the Roman Empire, Ravenna became capital of the territories the Eastern Roman Empire controlled in Italy from 553 to 751. Whereas San Vitale (532-548) displays the typical Byzantine church layout, with its central plan and domed roof, Sant'Apollinare in Classe (532-49) - like Sant'Apollinare Nuovo (490-549) – uses a typically Italian basilical plan. The church's exterior is defined by distinct structures in bare brick with roofs: single-light windows are inserted along the sides of the nave and aisles; the atrium in front of the entrance protrudes out from the longitudinal naves; and the cylindrical bell tower (built in a later period) is rendered less impos-

16-17 and 17 ■ Three aerial views show the Basilica of Sant'Apollinare, highlighting its early Christian basilical plan, divided into three naves of different heights without a transept, and with a polygonal apse. Note also the atrium in front of the façade and the cylindrical bell tower. The use of brick as a building material, left bare on the exterior, is typical of Ravenna's 5-6th century architecture.

ing by the single, two- and three-light windows arranged in succession from bottom to top. Upon entering the church, the visitor s immediately struck by the two majestic rows of columns – twelve on each side – with single trunks in veined Proconnesian marble and Corinthian capitals with acanthus leaf carving. The columns have dosserets (typical of Byzantine architecture) that support a sequence of round-arched arcades, above which the smooth surfaces of the central nave stretch out; they are interspersed by windows and were originally faced in precious marbles (which were removed in the 15th century). The sequence of round plates portraying Ravenna's archbishops was made in the 18th century. A wide triumphal arch, with a monumental staircase in front of it, leads to the apse area, which is also divided into three sections: either side of the polygonal apse are two apsidal chapels, the *prothesis* and the *diaconicon*. The large triumphal arch of the presbytery and the apsidal vault display an evocative mosaic cycle in the Byzantine style.

Location	Style	Surface area	Type	Built
RAVENNA (ITALY)	EARLY CHRISTIAN BYZANTINE	20,451.43 FT²	LONGITUDINAL PLAN	6TH-7TH CENTURIES

Above the triumphal arch, a medallion stands out with a half-portrait of Christ, flanked by the winged symbols of the four evangelists; in the lower register the two cities of Jerusalem and Bethlehem are symbolically depicted with jewel-encrusted city walls, through which the twelve apostles are leaving in the form of lambs. In the apsidal chapel is a description of the Transfiguration of Christ, done using symbolic figures: God the Father is represented by a haloed hand, Christ by a bejewelled cross, and the three apostles by lambs – with naturalistic half-length portraits of the prophets Elias and Moses; the same layout is found in the lower level. Here, in the center of a stylized landscape full of trees, flora and fauna, the figure of Ravenna's first bishop, St. Apollinare, is shown in prayer among his followers, who are also represented in the form of lambs.

18-19 ■ Inside, the three naves are divided by two rows of arches on columns with classical Corinthian acanthus-leaf capitals.

18 bottom ■ The apsidal vault is decorated with splendid 6th-century mosaics with strongly symbolic themes.

19 top ■ The round plates in the central nave were made in the 18th century and portray Ravenna's bishops.

19 bottom ■ The piers of the triumphal arch contain a mosaic cycle, of which a detail is shown here.

20-21 ■ The large triumphal arch in the presbytery has a prominent band with the symbols of the four evangelists: here we see the ox of Luke.

20 bottom ■ The man associated with Matthew, together with John's eagle, and Mark's lion, completes the series of the four evangelists.

21 bottom ■ In the center of the upper band, a medallion with a half-portrait of Christ stands out, surrounded by the four winged figures.

BASILICA OF
HAGIA SOPHIA

[ISTANBUL ■ TURKEY]

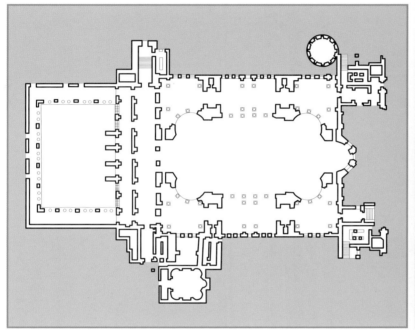

Known as "the great church" to Christians of the time, and dedicated to the Holy Wisdom, the Hagia Sophia was built by Emperor Justinian between 532 and 537, over the ruins of two earlier churches with a basilical plan. The emperor intended for it to become the most spectacular church in ancient Christendom; his wish was fulfilled, and the Hagia Sophia very quickly rose to become the ultimate symbol of Byzantine architecture. In order to achieve this, the finest builders and artisans were brought in from throughout the empire, while the governors of the provinces were asked to send their most precious marbles and stones to Constantinople.

For their part, Isidorus of Miletus and Anthemius of Tralles, the two architects and mathematicians who were assigned the task, defied the laws of statics and designed an extremely daring and original architectural structure: a double portal at the entrance leads into the church, which only appears to have a traditional basilical plan with a three-aisled nave (nevertheless of exceptional dimensions of 233 x 252.5 ft (71 x 77 m); in actual fact, the central nave is arranged as an ovoid centralized space with four enormous stone pillars (each measuring 25.1 x 59.8 ft/7.60 x 18.25 m) supporting a dome with

a diameter of over 105 ft (32 m), standing some 177 ft (54 m) above floor level. The vast square nave is separated from the side-aisles by a dramatic screen made up of two sequences of arched colonnades supporting the women's galleries above. Meanwhile, on the eastern and western sides, the space flows uninterruptedly beneath two enormous half domes at each end, which have the same diameter as the main dome and terminate in lower semi-circular apses, which are in turn screened off by columns. This structural solution, which was to become typical of Byzantine architecture, was possible thanks to what are known as pendentives. These are curved triangular joints that allow a dome to be placed above a square-plan building, thus avoiding the need for the continuous, thick walls which were required in Roman Imperial architecture to create the large vaulted spaces of public baths and basilicas. Vaulted structures were also created with slim bricks placed edgewise and drowned in thick beds of mortar

22 ■ The external walls of Hagia Sophia form a rectangular measuring 233 ft by 252 ft (71 x 77m). Inside a seemingly basilical plan with three naves and a polygonal apse is a centralized space dominated by the vast dome, supported by four stone pillars measuring 24.9 ft by 59.8 ft (7.60 x 18.25 m).

22-23 ■ This aerial view of the basilica, which is now a museum, highlights the breathtaking dimensions of the architectural complex.

Location	Style	Surface area	Type	Built
Istanbul (Turkey)	Byzantine	81,482.80 ft²	Centralized longitudinal plan	6th century

(up to 2.7 inches/7 cm high) so as to relieve the weight placed on the pillars. Perimeter walls were also made using the same technique, giving the entire building an extremely light appearance.

The sense of lightness and spatial expansion in the central area is emphasized by its covering of mosaics on a gold background; these reflect the light from the windows above the women's galleries, and especially from the twenty four open windows placed around the base of the dome which, symbolizing the vault of heaven, seems to hover in the air.

The only people to have access to the central nave, which was bathed in an ethereal splendor of light and color, would have been the clergy, guided by the patriarch, and the emperor accompanied by his court. The congregation, on the other hand, was confined to the side aisles and the galleries (women on one side, men on the other); the screens of columns, which may have been partly closed off with curtains,

24-25 ■ In this view of the large square nave above which the central dome rises, the apse can be seen in the background. In addition, at the sides are the screens of columns that separate the central nave from the side aisles and the tribune gallery.

24 bottom ■ The faithful could watch religious ceremonies from the large tribune galleries.

meant that they could only glimpse the magnificence of the central nave, which thus remained shrouded in mystery. The exterior architecture of the Hagia Sophia features solid structures surmounted by lead-covered domes, with a series of buttresses that were gradually added over time for the purposes of statics; four large minarets were added in 1453 when the Turks conquered Constantinople and the church was turned into a mosque. In 1923 Mustafà Kemal founded the Turkish Republic, and in 1934 converted the Hagia Sophia into a museum.

26-27 ■ In the center of the great dome, around the image of a sun, is an inscription with text taken from the Koran.

28 top and 29 ■ In the south gallery Christ is depicted between the Empress Zoe and her husband Constantine IX, while in the north gallery there is his intense image.

28 center and bottom ■ The tympanum on the door of the narthex is decorated with a mosaic showing the Virgin with Justinian and Constantine I. In the south gallery another portrait, of which we see a detail, depicts Mary between John II Comnenus and his wife Irene.

The complex historical events that led to the creation of the present Basilica of St. Mark began in 828; that year, two Venetian merchants smuggled the relics of St. Mark the Evangelist out of Alexandria in Egypt, in the tradition of "sacred theft" which was widespread at the time. The following year, in his bequest the Doge Giustiniano Particiaco (827-829) provided for the construction of a palatine chapel to hold the precious relics: the original church dedicated to St. Mark was built in an area adjacent to the Doge's Palace and was restored in 976 following a catastrophic fire. It was completely renovated in 1063 by the Doge Domenico Contarini (1043-1070), who wished to leave a lasting sign of his years in power.

ST. MARK'S
BASILICA

[VENICE ■ ITALY]

30-31 ■ The façade of St. Mark's highlights the glittering mosaic decorations on their golden background.

31 ■ The gilded bronze horses, from Contantinople, were placed above the lunette of the main portal during the rule of Doge Ranieri Zeno (1253-1268). In 1982, the originals were replaced with cast bronze copies.

32 top ■ The Porta della Carta, which leads from the basilica to the Doge's Palace. The winged lion was the emblem of the city dubbed la Serenissima.

33 ■ St. Mark's Square, surrounded by the porticoes of the Procuratie Vecchie and Procuratie Nuove, is a sort of vast public atrium for the basilica.

Recent historiographical information – obtained from excavations carried out in the 1990s – has indicated that the earlier church already had a Greek cross floor plan with five shallow domes; this contradicts the previous theory that it had a basilical floor plan with a three-aisled nave in the Early Christian tradition. The centralized floor plan was probably modeled on the church of the Twelve Apostles in Constantinople, which was built three centuries before St. Mark's Basilica. This reference to the long-standing, typically Byzantine architectural tradition reflects the strong political, commercial and cultural links that Venice had with the Eastern Roman Empire.

Doge Contarini's majestic basilica was completed in 1072, perhaps partly thanks to the contribution of an anonymous Byzantine architect. The building's structure is defined by a Greek cross plan above which are five domes – four on the arms of the cross and the fifth in the center; each dome is supported by four large barrel arches which discharge the weight onto as many four-footed pillars; the pillars in turn repeat, on a lesser scale, the same structural motif, as they consist of four piers joined together at two levels and ending in a small dome. The mighty pillars are also joined together by a sequence of arched colonnades that divide each arm of the cross, except for the presbytery, into three aisles, and support what were previously

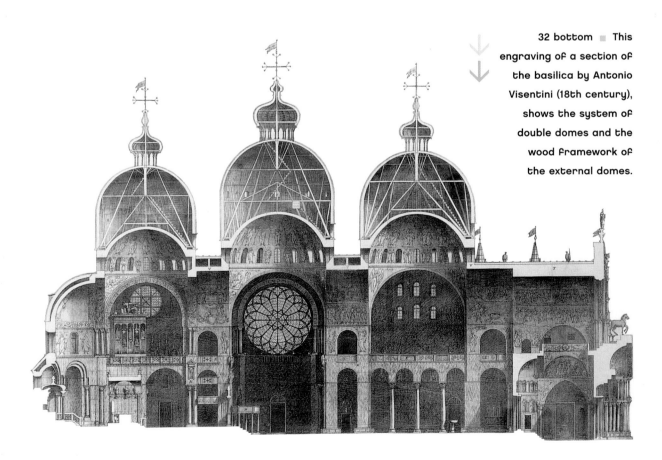

32 bottom ■ This engraving of a section of the basilica by Antonio Visentini (18th century), shows the system of double domes and the wood framework of the external domes.

34 ■ The baptistery, on the right side of the basilica, dates back to the rule of Doge Giovanni Soranzo (1312-1328): the baptismal font can be seen in the foreground.

the women's galleries (in the 12th and 13th centuries they were reduced to the present walkways). The center of the cross defines the space of the presbytery; here there is the High Altar with the marble sarcophagus that contains the relics of St. Mark. The presbytery is raised around 23.6 inches (60 cm) from ground level (beneath it lies the crypt; it is separated from the central nave by an imposing screen called an iconostasis (another typical feature of Byzantine architecture), and terminates in a semi-circular apse at its eastern end.

Inside the basilica, worshippers are immediately struck by the glittering mosaic decorations on a gold background. They were completed over eight centuries and completely cover the vaulted surfaces for over 43,055 sq. ft (4000 sq. m), forming a complex iconographic and theological cycle.

The building's exterior was also completed between the 13th and 15th centuries. Each of the five domes was covered with a second, higher dome, so that from the outside they took on their distinctive "onion" shape; meanwhile, the simple masonry of the façade was sumptuously embellished with marbles, columns, sculptures and mosaics, and topped off with a Gothic-style crown of pinnacle arches separated by niches. Upon its completion in the 17th century, the piazza in front of the basilica effectively provided a vast public atrium for the basilica itself; a typical theme of Early Christian and Byzantine architecture was thus achieved through a spectacular, unprecedented solution.

35 ■ In the foreground is one of the large arches that support the domes; in the background is the red marble iconostasis with polychrome panels that leads to the presbytery. All the surfaces above the marble cladding are covered with mosaics, which were intended to teach illiterate worshippers the lessons of the Bible.

Location	Style	Surface area	Type	Built
Venice (Italy)	Byzantine	26,672.97 ft²	Greek-cross plan	9th-14th centuries

TUFGNOEDAIMTIBE ETVOLVCBM/DISETMV DSEIEXOMI
DEVIR   CASICPCE

INARTICLODIEI INCRESSVS ENOESEM CHAME RAPHET

ATILIAVENITADEVPOTSRAMVOLNEIORE ETT
·PONAMARC

NOE OPTVLIT HOLOCVSTVDNO·   PDILVVIS

36 and 37 ■ The images show scenes from the story of
Noah. Splendid mosaics of the ark and the universal flood
cover some of the vaults in the narthex at the entrance
to the basilica (13th century). The mosaics in the atrium
narrate episodes from the Old Testament, while inside
they cover the main events of the life of Christ.

CATHEDRAL OF
ST. MARY THE VIRGIN

[PISA ■ ITALY]

According to the annals of history, the decision to rebuild Pisa Cathedral was made the day after the Pisan navy's famous victory over the Saracens in Palermo (1063), in order to crown the seafaring republic's hegemony in the western Mediterranean with a major architectural construction. Begun by the renowned architect Buscheto in 1064 on the foundations of an earlier Longobard church (748), and consecrated by Pope Gelasius II in 1118, it did in fact become the largest Romanesque church in Tuscany.

What makes it so original is its combination of Early Christian derived elements – the basilical floor plan, the women's gallery, the pitched roof above the nave – with Byzantine motifs (the mosaic in the apsidal vault, and some of the capitals) and shapes of Islamic origin, such as the extradosed ogival dome. This synergy between the different cultures which thrived on the shores of the Mediterranean at that time led to a new, evocative architectural blend.

The floor plan is based on the juxtaposition of three "basilicas": the longitudinal body with five-aisled nave,

38 ■ The aerial view shows the architectural complex of the Campo dei Miracoli in the north-western corner of the medieval city: the vast green lawn contains the long structures of the Campo Santo and the Hospital, the circular buildings of the Baptistery and the Leaning Tower, and the Latin-cross structure of the cathedral.

39 ■ The cathedral dominates the Campo, with the Baptistery arranged on the axis of the façade (so that the two domes are aligned, and in the background to the right, the famous Leaning Tower.

ending in the apse, is crossed perpendicularly by the transept. Both arms of the transept form autonomous areas with three naves, and also terminate in an apse. At the focal point of this arrangement, the crossing of the three structures, stands the elliptical dome, which is framed by four pointed triumphal arches.

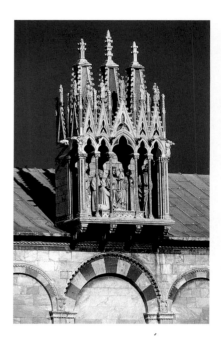

The walls of the central nave have a double order (also used in the transept): above a sequence of round-arched arcades supported by Roman-style columns is the women's gallery; this is defined by a sequence of two-light windows with a slim central column, which are separated by cruciform pillars placed above the columns below. The wall above, faced in stone, is pierced by a row of single-light windows that allow light into the central nave, which originally had wooden trusses but now has a 16th-century lacunar ceiling.

The cathedral's interior features alternate horizontal bands of white and black marble: this decorative element, which may have oriental origins, was to become typical of the Tuscan Romanesque style; for example, it is also found in the Basilica of San Miniato al Monte in Florence.

From 1100 onwards, architect Rainaldo began working on the cathedral. He was responsible for expanding the three bays of the nave section and, above all, designing the distinctive motif of the tiered loggias, with their lacy arcades and slim columns;

40 top ■ On the exterior of the cathedral is a Gothic-style tabernacle.

40 bottom left ■ Gargoyles for draining rainwater like this one are placed on the cathedral's main façade.

40 in bottom right ■ The gallery which encircles the base of the dome has pointed arches of typically Gothic design resting on slim columns. It was added in the 14th century.

41 ■ The upper part of the cathedral's façade is defined by the distinctive motif of tiered loggias which screen off, for a lighter effect, the blind wall of the façade behind.

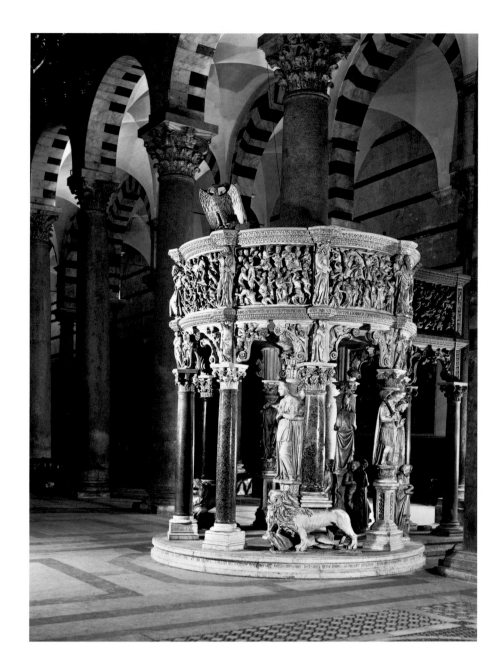

this motif defines the architecture of the façade (as well as the apse area), creating an elegant effect of lightness and transparency.

The cathedral is part of an extraordinary, unique monumental complex which is considered one of the greatest masterpieces of Italian architecture – the Piazza dei Miracoli – and also includes the Baptistery (Diotisalvi and Nicola Pisano, 1153-1265), the Leaning Tower (Bonanno, 1174-1271), the Campo Santo and the Hospital (Giovanni di Simone, 13th century). The cathedral is the pivot around which this vast urban space is arranged: the circular Baptistery (the diameter of which is equal to the width of the church's five aisles) is aligned on the axis of the façade; meanwhile on the opposite side, slightly to one side of the apse, stands the Leaning Tower, also circular. Both buildings take up the subtle play of variations and chiaroscuro effects of the tiered loggia motif found in the cathedral.

The Leaning Tower began to tilt even before it had been completed; the repetition of the colonnade motif completely covers the whole building, so much so that the German scholar and historian Rudolf Borchardt perceptively described it as a "column of columns."

42 ■ The famous marble pulpit by Giovanni Pisano (1302-1310) is situated in the central nave.

43 ■ This view of the central nave clearly shows the sequences of arched colonnades that border it, supporting the tribune gallery level above and framing the large ogival arch.

CATHEDRAL OF THE
NATIVITY
OF MARY

[MONREALE ▪ ITALY]

44 ▪ The apsidal area has Islamic motifs, carried out by
local Arab craftsmen.

44-45 ▪ The architectural complex of Monreale stands on
the slopes of Monte Caputo, 4.3 miles (7 km) from Palermo.
The cathedral has a basilical plan, and is flanked on the south
by the large cloister of the adjacent Benedictine monastery.

The monumental complex of Monreale consists of the cathedral with an attached monastery, the royal palace and the archbishop's palace. It was built from 1174 onwards, by King William II; his aim was to carry out a vast building project that would express the power of the new Norman dynasty. Norman knights and armies had driven the Arabs out of Sicily in 1091, and the new Normans re-established Christianity on the island, and then went on to found the Kingdom of Naples and Sicily in 1130.

The atmosphere of political stability had been regained, and the new dynasty showed an interest in various forms of artistic expression; this led to a period in which Sicilian architecture flourished. Local motifs derived from the Islamic and Byzantine styles were incorporated into the Early Christian tradition and Norman elements; the result was that in Palermo masterpieces were built such as the Palatine Chapel (1132-1140), the church of San Giovanni degli Eremiti (1132), the palaces of La Zisa (1154-1166) and La Cubo (1180). However, the largest and most important church was indeed the Duomo of Monreale, built

on high ground from which it dominates the bay of Palermo. The building has a Latin cross basilical plan with a non-projecting transept, clearly derived from the Early Christian tradition: a nave and side aisles with timber roofs are divided by two rows of nine columns, mainly from the Roman era; they support a sequence of arches. Above these is the wall, interspersed with large windows that shed light onto the nave. Typically Islamic features are included in this structure, such as the ogival shape of the arches; the polychromatic geometric decoration of the timber ceiling (reconstructed between 1816-37, following the original design); the stylized stalactite motif on the ceiling above the crossing. Meanwhile, the so-called dosserets derive from the Byzantine culture: inverted pyramid-sections placed between the capitals and the

46 top 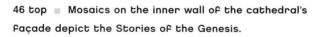 Mosaics on the inner wall of the cathedral's façade depict the Stories of the Genesis.

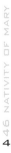

46 bottom ■ The columns in the central nave, from spolia materials, support Islamic style ogival arches.

46-47 ■ The mosaic in the apsidal vault is dominated by the imposing figure of Christ Pantocrator (Jesus Christ the Omnipotent).

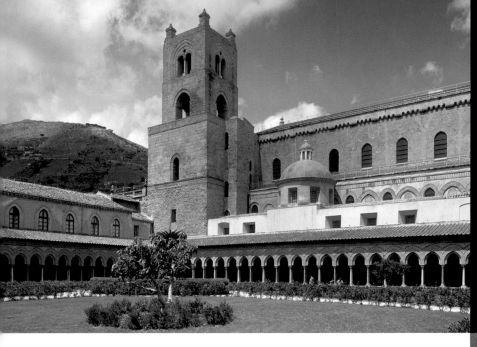

arches, which widen the bearing surface of the capitals. However, more than anything it is the splendid mosaic decorations on a gold background that uninterruptedly cover the entire surface area of 68,243 sq. ft (6340 sq. m) that give the interior its awe-inspiring atmosphere and immediately provoke an emotional response.

Scholars believe that teams of master mosaic artists from Byzantium executed the mosaic cycle. It was made with a precise narrative purpose in mind: the sections go through the Holy Bible, starting with the crucial events the Old Testament, which are shown on the walls of the nave; it then continues in the transept and choir with scenes from the lives of the saints, the apostles and Jesus; it then culminates in the apsidal vault with the striking figure of Christ Pantocrator (Jesus the Omnipotent). Furthermore, the path followed by the faithful from the cathedral entrance to the apsidal area symbolizes the path that each of us has to follow to reach eternal salvation.

The cathedral's exterior also features a perfect blend of various visual elements: while the main façade is flanked by two Norman-style towers (the portico in front dates from the 18th century), the interlacing arch decoration is typically Arab; this is also found in the structures of the apse area, which are decorated with fine interlacing ogival arches and enriched with inlaid motifs in polychromatic stone. All that remains intact of the ancient Benedictine monastery is the large cloister (154 sq. ft /47 sq. m), a quadrangle next to the southern side of the cathedral. Its highly original architecture features 228 slender twin columns supporting pointed arches decorated with geometric designs. The columns – some of which have mosaic inlays, others carved with arabesques – feature a rich variety of carved capitals. The same motifs are repeated in the southwestern corner, in an elegant, square cloister-within-a-cloister with a fountain at its center.

LOCATION	STYLE	SURFACE AREA	TYPE	BUILT
MONREALE (ITALY)	BYZANTINE-ROMANESQUE	43,055.64 FT²	LATIN-CROSS PLAN	12TH CENTURY

48 and 49 ■ Construction of the Benedictine abbey began in 1175, with a square plan of 154 ft (47 m) on each side Four porticoes, each with 26 Islamic-style ogival arches, enclose the internal garden. The arches are supported by slender twin columns

with are decorated with mosaics on the shafts and capitals. The fountain in the small cloister (top right) has a palm-shaped column standing in a round pool. Water spurts in small jets from the mouths of sculpted people and lions.

49 NATIVITY OF MARY

ST. STEPHEN'S
CATHEDRAL

[SPEYER ■ GERMANY]

Speyer Cathedral is one of the masterpieces of the German Romanesque style. It is remarkable for its vast dimensions – its overall length is 436.3 ft (133 m) and the main nave alone is 49.2 ft (15 m) wide, while the transept measures 180.4 ft (55 m) overall – as well as for its design; it displays an innovative, somber unity of the motifs which would come to symbolize Romanesque architecture. Indeed, at Speyer Cathedral the wall was no longer used as a canvas for cycles of paintings as it had been in the Ottonian period; (ca. 960-1060) instead it became a point of interest in itself due to the addition of different levels, overhangs and protrusions that make it a veritable "sculpted mass." The frescoes in the main nave were in fact added in the 19th century. The cathedral was begun in 1030 during the reign of the Emperor Conrad II (1027-1039, and was finished by Henry IV (1056-1105) in 1066. Twenty years later, changes were made to it, perhaps due to its diminished stability after flooding from the Rhine. The general layout of the church dates from its first stage of construc-

50 ■ The repetition of elevated rounded arcades gives rhythm to the external surface of the church.

50-51 ■ This aerial view shows the Westwerk, which was the emperor's loggia and was turned into an entrance porch for the church in the 19th century; beyond it is the longitudinal body of the church with the transept, from which rises the drum and octagonal dome.

tion. It consists of a three-aisled nave, the crypt beneath the presbytery, the crossing, the transept and the Westwerk (a loggia for the Emperor's use, enclosed between two towers and placed in front of the longitudinal body of the church). At the sides of the transept are two smaller chapels: the Emmers Kapelle, which has a square floor plan divided by four columns; and the Afrakapelle, which was rebuilt in the 19th century.

Inside the building, the masonry takes on greater volume and depth, and is modeled by tiers in relief which appear again in the structure of the tall, square pillars in the central nave. Half-columns are in fact placed against these pillars, highlighting the vertical dimension of the nave, which is further accentuated by the lack of a tribune gallery. The half-columns continue alongside the pillars as far as the intrados of the ceiling; they alternate a double order placed over a "giant order" that was before its time. This generates the sequence of vertical uprights according to an A-b-A-b-A rhythm which reflects the alternation of the bays in the side-aisles with the bays in the main nave. The latter was covered with quadri-partite vaults in 1080, during the second phase of construction; this phase involved the removal of the trussed ceiling, the strengthening of the pillars and the enlargement of the transept and semi-circular apse, which became the same width as the central nave. Externally, the apse is flanked by two square towers and has tall blind arcades, above which is a light arcaded gallery; this is repeated in the end portions of the transept and the side-aisles. The crypt beneath the apse repeats the layout of the cathedral on a smaller scale; it replicates the three apsidal naves and the transept, supported by sturdy yet elegant columns with capitals and dosserets. Several German emperors were buried here, including the founders of the church, from Conrad II to Henry IV, as well as the wife and daughter of Frederick Barbarossa. Lastly, in the 19th century the architect Heinrich Hübschs turned the Westwerk into an entrance portico; from it emerge the end portions of the twin towers that originally embellished the façades of most Norman churches.

52 top ■ It is said that King Rudolph I (1218-1291), the Holy Roman Emperor whose tombstone is shown here, wanted to return to Speyer when he was about to die.

52 bottom left ■ The crypt stands on solid columns with capitals and dosserets. It is divided into three naves, like the church above it.

52 bottom right ■ The Emmeramskapelle, dedicated to St. Martin and also used as a baptismal chapel, was begun in 1050.

53 ■ The wide central nave runs between an uninterrupted sequence of half-columns placed against pillars, which culminates in a solid round arch at the crossing with the transept.

Location	Style	Surface area	Type	Built
Speyer (Germany)	Romanesque	71,041.81 ft²	Longitudinal plan	11th-12th centuries

CHRIST'S

CATHEDRAL

[DURHAM ■ UNITED KINGDOM]

"Grey Towers of Durham, Yet well I love thy mixed and massive piles. Half church of God, half castle 'gainst Scot."

With these words, Sir Walter Scott captures the essence of the towered, sturdy cathedral with a Benedictine monastery attached, which rises above the lush vegetation of the loop of the River Wear. It has ancient origins linked to St. Cuthbert, the most venerated saint in northeast England. Cuthbert lived in the 7th century and became a monk after seeing a vision; he was buried in the church of Lindisfarne.

When his body was exhumed a decade later, it showed no signs of decay, and so it was placed in a reliquary and displayed to worshippers. Danish incursions into England forced the monks to leave Lindisfarne and seek out a new place for their convent and for the saint's mortal remains; at last, in 995 they chose the safety and quiet of the banks of the River Wear, where they initially built a wooden sanctuary, and later built a church called White Church.

In 1093, Bishop William de St. Carileph began work on the current structure, which was built to hold the relics of St. Cuthbert and was completed in 1133; the chapterhouse, the Galilee Chapel, the Chapel of the Nine Altars and the High Altar with the Neville altar-frontal were added later on. The bell tower was built in the second half of the 15th century, thus completing a design that is clearly Anglo-Norman in style. Indeed, the long three-aisled nave section is broken by a transept placed just beyond its halfway point, after which stands the iconostasis which separates it from the presbytery. The sequence of rectangular bays follows the strict A-b-A-b-A system; it alternates sturdy cylindrical stone pillars carved with deep geometric grooves, placed by the bays of the side-aisles, with cluster pillars that rise uninterrupted to support the ribbed cross vaults in the nave. The relief ribbing of the vaults therefore concludes the upwards thrust of the pillars, unifying the interior space of the nave in a strictly linear design that anticipates the Gothic structural skeleton.

The pillars are connected by a sequence of round arches which is repeated in the triforium and the clerestory, framed by the lunettes in the vaults. The transept has a narrow transverse aisle out of which two chapels are formed; above the square crossing rises the imposing bell tower, which has a lantern of about 1574 ft (48 m) in height, topped with a flat roof. It is taller and more imposing than the two towers that stand on either side of the cathedral's façade. The façade was altered with the addition of the Galilee Chapel at the end of the 12th

55 ■ **This aerial view of Durham Cathedral offers a sweeping look over the entire architectural complex. Annexed to the longitudinal body of the church are the Chapter House, the cloister and other monastic buildings.**

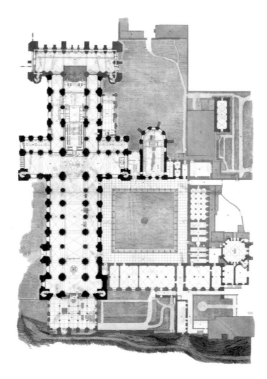

56 top ■ The plan clearly depicts the cathedral's layout; in sequence are the Galilee Chapel, the two towers of the façade, the main nave, the transept, the choir and the Chapel of Nine Altars, which coincides with the apse are. Adjacent to the cathedral is the cloister.

century. The chapel contains the tomb of the Venerable Bede, author of the *Ecclesiastical History of England*; meanwhile the entrance to the cathedral was moved to the left side, on Palace Green.

At the end of the 13th century the three original semi-circular apses were replaced to allow for the building of the Chapel of the Nine Altars. The chapel has a lighter look due to the appearance of the first Gothic features; these are accentuated by the level of the floor, which is lower than the rest of the church. The Norman cloister dating from the same time was altered considerably in the following period. Durham Cathedral is now acknowledged as one of the masterpieces of English Norman architecture. It is dedicated to Christ, the Virgin Mary and St. Cuthbert.

56 bottom ■ The episcopal throne is situated above the tomb and chantry chapel of Bishop Hatfield (1345-1381), and was placed there in his memory.

56-57 ■ In the central nave, there is a distinct alternation between cylindrical pillars and cluster pillars. The iconostasis is in the background.

→ →

Location	Style	Surface area	Type	Built
Durham (United Kingdom)	Romanesque-Gothic	63,507.07 ft²	Longitudinal plan	11th-15th centuries

CATHEDRAL OF THE

HOLY AND UNDIVIDED TRINITY

[ELY ▪ UNITED KINGDOM]

Ely Cathedral is a spectacular building that was begun in the Norman period and completed in the 14th century. It owes its appeal to the layering of various architectural styles from the different phases of the Romanesque and Gothic periods, which can be identified by observing the individual parts of the building. The cathedral has a very long-established history. In the 7th century, the Saxon princess Etheldreda was forced to marry; however, she later fled, taking refuge on her own land in Ely where she founded a monastery for monks and nuns. The monastery was destroyed by the Danes, and was later rebuilt by a Benedictine community in the year 970 together with the church; the body of St. Etheldreda was incredibly well preserved, and was placed in a reliquary and displayed to worshippers. In 1083, on a site not far from the River Ouse, work began on the current building, which was finished in Norman style in 1189. In this first phase the three-aisled nave and the transepts were built, while the Galilee Porch and presbytery already show some Early English features. The Lady Chapel was added between the 14th and 15th centuries; also in this period, the octagon of the crossing was rebuilt and the choir was expanded, both featuring elements of the Decorated Style.

58 ▪ This view of the south side of the cathedral shows, in sequence, the remaining section of the entrance transept, the side of the cathedral and the north transept; above the latter rises the tower that stands above the octagon of the crossing.

59 ▪ In the center of the front of the cathedral is the west entrance, the Galilee Porch, with the West Tower above it. To the right stands the surviving wing of the entrance transept, with its distinctive turrets; the main transept and the Lady Chapel can be seen in the background on the left.

60 top ■ The tomb and chantry chapel of Bishop Redman (1501-1505), renowned for his generosity toward the poor. It is richly decorated with sculptures referring to the Passion of Christ, and is a fine example of the Perpendicular Style.

60 bottom ■ An effigy of Alan of Walsingham is sculpted into the north-east arch impost at the base of the octagon at the crossing.

61 ■ The massive Norman pillars in the nave rise up to the wooden ceiling which was added by Sir Gilbert Scott in the 19th century; they are approximately 22 meters high.

The main façade is Norman and is dominated by the imposing West Tower, which stands some 216.5 ft (66 m) in height. The façade has an asymmetrical appearance since originally it formed an actual transept providing access to the cathedral; the north part of this has disappeared, but the remaining section, with two octagonal towers with rows of arcading, is remarkably beautiful. The church is entered through the Galilee Porch, an addition to the façade, which leads into the nave; the latter, flanked by side-aisles, is some 249.3 (76 m) in length, while the church's overall length is 538 ft (164 m). The cathedral's interior is striking for the vertical sequence of a triple order of round arches on cluster pillars that underline their height, from floor level right up to the clerestory. The rhythm of this sequence is interrupted at the crossing with the transept where the wooden ceiling, added by Sir George Gilbert Scott in the 19th century, finishes in a tall pointed arch, which is proof of the change of period. This becomes even more evident with the series of blind arcades on slender columns in the southwest transept; from the center, they become gradually more pointed, moving from Romanesque to Early English. The finish of the stonework indicates that most of the arches in the nave would have been colored, although today only a few traces of color remain. Beyond the crossing, the choir is characterized by the appearance of the Decorated Style. This style is also found in the Lady Chapel, which dates from the same period; the Lady Chapel was the largest to be built in an English church in the 13th and 14th centuries. Lastly, the octagonal tower above the crossing was built from 1322 onwards after the previous tower collapsed; it is 75.4 ft (23 m) wide and stands on eight stone piers leading into strips of slim ribs which define the impost of the lantern. These ribs conceal the wooden framework that supports the lantern. The monks commissioned William Hurley, the king's own carpenter, to do this work. It is a particularly complex structure and around 220 tons (200 tonnes) of timber, lead and glass were used to make it; the ribs on the vaults form a star-shaped surface. The interior is lit by four windows placed on the diagonal sides, in the same way as in the octagonal tower below. The lantern was restored in the 1990s, thus completing the structural renovation work that began in 1986 following a public appeal for the building's conservation. The monastic buildings are now used by the King's School and by members of the Ely Cathedral community.

Location	Style	Surface area	Type	Built
Ely (United Kingdom)	Romanesque-Gothic	45,977.48 ft²	Longitudinal plan	11th – 14th centuries

BASILICA OF
SAINTE MADELEINE

[VÉZELAY ▪ FRANCE]

In medieval times, the monastery of Vézelay – which was already a meeting place for pilgrims on the road to Santiago de Compostela – was the setting for significant historical events related to the conquest of sacred Christian sites in the Holy Land. On 31 March 1146, St. Bernard of Clairvaux preached in favor of the Second Crusade; then in July 1190 English and French armies met at the monastery before leaving for the Third Crusade, led by the monarchs Richard the Lionheart of England and Philip Augustus of France. The Benedictine abbey church is still situated in a picturesque environment: high on a hill, it overlooks the hilly Burgundy landscape with the old town of Vézelay beneath it. The Basilica is reputed to house the holy relics of Mary Magdalene; construction began in 1096 and progressed so

62-63 ■ This aerial view shows the town of Vézelay in the foreground and, in the background, the hilly landscape of Burgundy. The basilica and hill were added to the World Heritage List in 1979.

63 ■ This watercolor by Eugène E. Viollet-le-Duc (1840) shows the state of the façade before the restoration work he himself carried out, commissioned by the famous writer Prosper Mérimée.

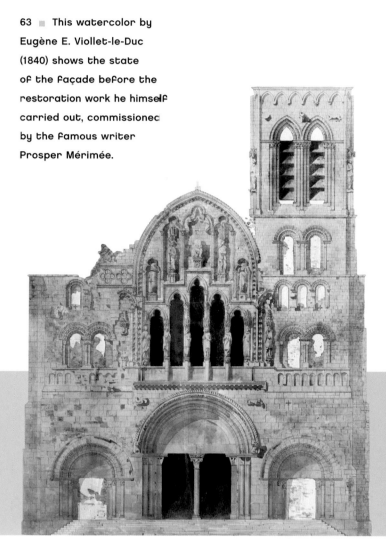

swiftly that by the beginning of the 12th century the choir area and the nave and aisles had already been completed; however, the latter were then rebuilt a century later in the years 1220-40 because of a serious fire which destroyed the church's longitudinal body. Meanwhile, the choir with its ambulatory and radiating chapels, and the transept bays were rebuilt at the end of the 12th century following the new dictates of the Gothic style. This is why the architecture at Vézelay is considered one of the foremost examples of the evolution from Romanesque to Gothic forms within the same building.

The basilica has a longitudinal body with a narthex, a slightly projecting transept and a choir with five radiating chapels; beneath the presbytery area is a large Carolingian crypt with low, sturdy cross vaulting supported by 12 columns. The building is remarkable for its length, defined by a sequence of 13 bays in the long, narrow triple-aisled nave (some 205 ft/62.5 m in length). The rectangular bays of the nave are matched by square bays in the side-aisles. Above the nave, which is higher than the side-aisles, are cross vaults on cluster pillars; corresponding to each bay, the pillars are spaced with monumental round transverse arches built with black and white ashlars. The elevation is on two levels, without a tribune; the round-arched arcade which separates the nave from the side-aisles is followed by a brick wall pierced by a sequence of single-light windows that let light into the nave. The

Location	Style	Surface area	Type	Built
Vézelay (France)	Romanesque-Gothic	37,673.69 ft²	Longitudinal plan	11th-12th centuries

←→

64-65 ■ The bas-relief decoration in the central portal of the narthex welcomes believers into the basilica. The area of the Gothic choir is visible in the background, with ogival arches and windows that let light flood onto the altar.

65 top ■ In the nave, a regular sequence of round-arched arcades borders the cross vaults, which are placed above rectangular bays and supported by cluster pillars.

bas-relief carved into the tympanum in the central portal of the narthex boasts particularly fine craftsmanship and is considered one of the masterpieces of French Romanesque architecture: Christ on a throne is surrounded by the apostles; in a semi-circle around them are the first peoples to be evangelized, while below, on the architrave, are the peoples who rejected or ignored the Gospel. In the lower part of the façade are three typically Romanesque portals with slender piers and wide, shallow round arches. In the upper portion, a large window with five very narrow lancets of varying heights is surmounted by a large ogival arch, flanked by two towers of different heights. The bas-relief portraying the Last Judgment in the tympanum of the central portal was reconstructed in the 19th century. Indeed, another fire, this time in 1819, marked the history of the basilica of Vézelay; it led to a major restoration project led by the architect Eugène Viollet-le-Duc between 1840-1859.

65 bottom ■ The capitals display the full range of figurative themes that were typical of the medieval doctrinal and allegorical culture: fantastical or monstrous animals, human figures busy doing everyday tasks and stylized plants and flowers.

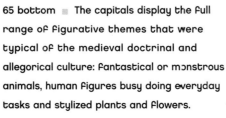

CATHEDRAL OF
NOTRE-DAME

[PARIS ■ FRANCE]

In 1163 Bishop Maurice de Sully ordered the building of the cathedral of Notre-Dame to be commenced; he decided to radically transform the ancient basilica of Saint-Étienne, which by that time was considered out of date, according to the new canons of Gothic architecture which were spreading throughout northern France.

The ambitious bishop wanted the cathedral to be over 416.6 ft (127 m) long and 131.2 ft (40 m) wide; its construction required complex engineering work to be carried out so that the surface area of the Île de la Cité could be increased by incorporating a small island rising alongside it. The changes to the area's town planning were then completed with the construction of an immense sacristy and the opening of a road leading to the cathedral. This road measured some 19.6 (6 m) in width: these dimensions were unprecedented in an age in which the existing urban fabric was remarkably dense. The floor plan of Notre-Dame is

←→

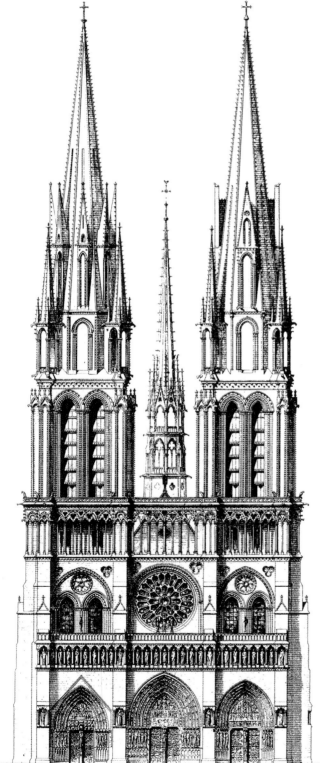

68 ■ In this engraving, Eugène E. Viollet-le-Duc, who was commissioned by J.B. Lassus to restore the building between 1847-1864, gives an idea of how the cathedral would look if it had been completed with the two spires above the towers (which were planned but never built) and the third spire above the crossing (destroyed in 1792).

69 ■ The façade of Notre-Dame has an extremely rigorous composition which reflects the organization of the space within it. Note the large central rose window, 13 metres in diameter, which was to become the emblem of the European Gothic.

divided into five aisles, comprising a wide central nave; double side-aisles which continue through the presbytery and curve into the choir; a non-projecting transept; and a sequence of chapels around the side-aisles and the chevet (these were added from 1240 onwards). Each rectangular bay of the central nave is matched by two square bays in the side-aisles. The cross vaults in the central nave are thus sexpartite and reach a height of over 105 ft (32 m), making Notre-Dame the tallest church in Christendom in the 12th century.

The elevation of the nave is defined by a framework of architectural elements that mark out the wall: vertically, the sequence of cylindrical pillars is taken up by slim smaller columns that join the ribbing of the cross vaults in the nave and rest on the Corinthian-style capitals of the pillars. Horizontally, the elevation has a sequence of three tiers (originally four; they were reduced to three between 1220-30, modeled on Chartres Cathedral): on the first tier, the cylindrical pillars support ogival arches; on the second tier, which corresponds to the tribune gallery behind it, ogival arches are arranged into three-light windows; on the third tier – what is known as the clerestory – large two-light windows with a rose window above let light into the nave, which is not particularly bright, however, due to the addition of the side chapels.

The exterior of the cathedral is an imposing cruciform construction defined by the taller elements of the transept and the nave. The latter, including the chevet, is surrounded on three sides by a system of counterforts and flying buttresses which ensure the building's stability and allow large windows to be inserted in the clerestory and the choir.

A spire over 298.5 ft (91 m) tall, rebuilt by Eugène E. Viollet-le-Duc in Gothic style in the 19th century, rises above the crossing between the nave and transept.

70 ■ In this aerial view of the apsidal section, one can admire the circular termination of the chevet, which is underlined by the radiating arrangement of the flying buttresses.

70-71 ■ This view clearly shows the cross shape formed by the nave and the transept, and the system of flying buttresses which transmit the thrust of the main nave onto the buttresses.

LOCATION	STYLE	SURFACE AREA	TYPE	BUILT
PARIS (FRANCE)	GOTHIC	64,583.46 FT²	LONGITUDINAL PLAN	12TH-13TH CENTURIES

71 bottom ▪ The external walls of
the cathedral display various sculptural
elements that are typical of the Gothic
figurative universe.

72 ■ Light filtering through the stained glass of the large clerestory windows helps to create an evocative "supernatural" atmosphere.

73 ■ This general view of the nave shows the choir in the foreground and, in the background, the large rose window on the main façade.

74-75 ■ This picturesque night-time view shows off the Cathedral of Notre-Dame, with the chevet in the foreground, set into the urban landscape of Paris.

The two transept façades were rebuilt in the 13th century to align them with the side chapels; they are considered masterpieces of the so-called *rayonnant* style, due to the radiating design of the tracery in the large rose windows in their elevations.

The main façade was built in the early 13th century. It stands out for the clarity of its architectural layout, which takes up the design of the interior: the vertical division into three equal units corresponds to the layout of the nave and aisles, whereby the middle part corresponds to the main nave while the side parts correspond to the side-aisles, reflecting their double sequence in the large two-light windows in the middle portion of the façade and the two towers.

The horizontal arrangement of the façade is equally precise; its transenna is particularly light and elegant, with its tracery of crossed narrow arches on slender columns placed between the great rose window (42.6 ft/13 m in diameter) and the towers either side.

CATHEDRAL OF
NOTRE-DAME

[CHARTRES ■ FRANCE]

Chartres Cathedral rose on the ashes of a previous Romanesque church built in the 11th century, which was almost completely destroyed by a disastrous fire on 10 July 1194. The sacred relic kept in the original church – the tunic worn by Mary at the birth of Christ – escaped the fire unscathed. This fact was interpreted as a miraculous event, and encouraged the clergy as well as the nobility, the people and even the king himself to make a contribution to ensure that work could begin immediately on the new cathedral. The building work proceeded at a rapid pace, and was completed by the year 1230. The new cathedral at Chartres became the most noteworthy and majestic Marian sanctuary in the kingdom of France.

The building has a layout divided into three aisles, a projecting transept which in turn is also divided into three aisles, a chevet with five aisles and a choir with a double ambulatory and seven radiating chapels.

76 ■ The Royal Portal was the first of the major sculpture cycles of the Gothic period. The figures are arranged according to a precise iconographic system: the column-statues represent characters from the Old Testament; the capitals narrate the life of Christ; while the archivolts depict the liberal arts, the signs of the zodiac and the Labors of the Months.

77 ■ The Façade of Chartres cathedral is dominated by two towers topped with spires, by the large central rose window and by the Royal Portal.

Unlike in previous cathedrals, there is a perfect correspondence between the different bays: each rectangular bay unit in the central naves corresponds to a square bay unit in the side-aisles. All of the vaults are quadripartite while the pillars are cluster pillars with slender columns that blend into the ribbing of the cross vaults.

Other innovations in the cathedral are that the women's galleries are eliminated, the elevation of the nave is divided into three tiers, and the glass windows of the clerestory are extended. Indeed, the sequence of pillars on ogival arcades is followed by a low gallery of arches on slender columns – the triforium – and then by the *clair étage* level, which is structured into two-light windows with polylobed rose windows above them. The height of the clerestory is the same as that of the lower arcade, giving the elevation of the central nave precise proportional ratios for the first time. The same sequence is repeated in the transept and the choir, which is flooded with light due to the large number of windows and its own centric form.

All of these features enhance the verticality of the central nave – the ogival vaults reach a height of 124.6 ft (38 m) – and also help to increase the light in the interior. In fact the cathedral has some 173 windows almost all of which

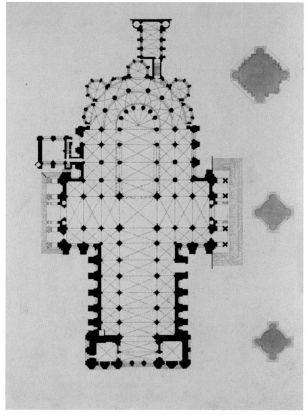

78-79 ■ This general view of Chartres Cathedral highlights the two spires of the façade, the South Portal and the chevet area with its imposing flying buttresses.

79 top ■ The flying buttresses have a distinctive shape that helps improve their static function.

79 bottom ■ This plan of the cathedral – drawn in the 19th century by Daniel Ramée – shows the division of the inner space, in which the chevet area is particularly complex, with its double ambulatory and radiating chapels.

Location	Style	Surface area	Type	Built
Chartres (France)	Gothic	75,320 ft²	Longitudinal plan	12th-13th centuries

have survived intact; together they total over 21,528 sq. ft (2000 sq. m); the main colors used are ruby red, dark blue and purple. The exterior of Chartres cathedral is remarkable for the architects' ability to give the system of flying buttresses a clearly defined architectural expression. Three flying buttresses are placed one above the other; the lower two are joined by a wheel motif created using small arcades on radiating columns that link each buttress to its corresponding pillar in the side-aisle.

The original design provided for nine towers, none of which was ever built. In fact, the two towers that dominate the main façade date back to the previous building; in particular, the northwestern tower, which was unfinished, was completed in 1507 and crowned with a spire in the Flamboyant style.

Meanwhile, the façades of the transepts date from the 13th century and contain a stunning cycle of sculptures (with over 90 statues) arranged according to a very strict order. As the sanctuary was a place of pilgrimage, unlike in other cathedrals these façades have three vast entrance portals in addition to those on the main nave.

Chartres Cathedral became the blueprint for cathedrals built in the following years, not only in the Île-de-France region but in the whole of Europe.

← ← 80-81 ■ This view shows, in sequence, the choir reserved for the clergy, the altar, the main nave for the worshippers and lastly, the huge rose window and three single-light windows on the façade.

81 top ■ This view of the nave highlights the large windows in the clerestory and choir which let light into the nave itself and the chevet. Note also the massive cluster pillars and the sequence of ogival arcades.

81 bottom ■ This photograph shows an elegant screen embellished with sculpture groups and typically Gothic traceries

82 and 83 ■ Two details of the 173 glass windows in Chartres Cathedral. In particular, the figure on the right shows King David with his harp.

CATHEDRAL OF
NOTRE-DAME

[AMIENS ▪ FRANCE]

Amiens Cathedral was built starting in 1220, by order of Bishop Richard de Gerberoy. He decided to demolish the previous Romanesque church (1152-1218), which had been damaged by fire, and build a cathedral big enough to receive the large number of pilgrims who flocked to see the relics that the Crusaders had brought back from the Holy Land in 1206. Driven by practical necessity and by the desire to emulate the great cathedrals that had been built in other French cities, the bishop commissioned the architect Robert de Luzarches to built a majestic building. The cathedral did in fact become the largest French medieval building.

The tight-knit urban fabric of the town meant that, unlike the usual procedure, construction had to begin from the façade; this was followed by the nave, the choir – built in the 1260s by Regnault de Cormont who took over from his father Thomas – and lastly the transept.

Several sources report that the work was completed in 1264, just 44 years after the first stone was laid; this was made possible by the rationalization of building methods and by the immense financial resources plowed

84 ▪ The façade of Amiens Cathedral repeats, with some variations, the same compositional layout of Notre-Dame in Paris. There is an impressive abundance of decorative and sculptural elements.

85 ▪ This image shows a detail of the façade with the Gallery of the Kings and the large central rose window.

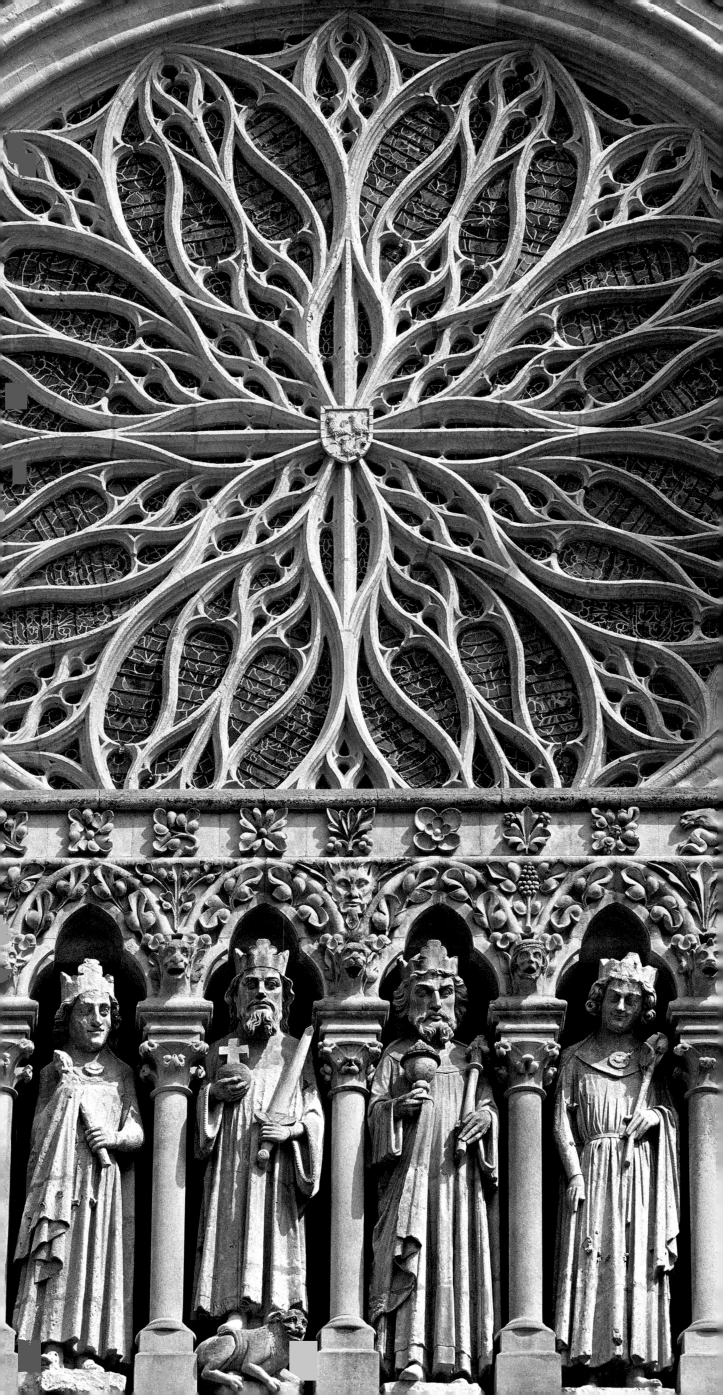

into the project. The building was undoubtedly modeled on Chartres Cathedral: the layout is a Latin cross floor plan with a three-aisled nave as far as the transept, which is in turn divided into three. The chevet (the eastern termination of the apse) is divided into five aisles; meanwhile the choir, unlike that at Chartres, has a single ambulatory and is surrounded by seven radiating chapels, six of which are identical, with a deeper central chapel dedicated to the Virgin Mary. This solution became very popular and was also used in several English cathedrals. The later construction of chapels between the buttresses of the side-aisles aligned the longitudinal body with the chevet.

The elevation is also organized according to the three-tiered layout used for the first time in Chartres Cathedral; here, however, some innovations are introduced, related to the doubled rhythm: the triforium level is placed above a sequence of ogival arches on cluster pillars; for each bay unit it has two three-light windows topped by trefoils. For each bay unit, the clerestory level has two two-light windows with tracery above, enclosed within an ogival arch which contains a small rose window. This solution results in a larger area of glazed surfaces, developing the process typical of Gothic architecture whereby the wall is broken up and considered as a glass surface furrowed by a very fine stone framework. This style was later taken to extremes in Sainte-Chapelle in Paris.

86-87 ■ This atmospheric view of the cathedral's interior, at the crossing between the nave and transept, highlights the ceiling system, which consists of quadripartite and sexpartite ribbed vaults.

87 ■ These pictures show opposing views of the nave, highlighting the large windows in the choir and the rose window on the west façade. Note the sobriety of the inner space, contrasting with the opulence of the exterior.

Location	Style	Surface area	Type	Built
AMIENS (FRANCE)	GOTHIC	82,882.11 FT²	LONGITUDINAL PLAN	13TH CENTURY

The Amiens architects then took the cross vaults of the main nave even further upwards, reaching a height of over 137.7 ft/42 m (compared to 131.2 ft/40 m at Rheims and 124.6 ft/38 m at Chartres), in an almost obsessive competition to build the tallest cathedral possible, defying the technical capabilities of the time.

The façade takes up the typical tripartite arrangement that was first used in Notre-Dame in Paris, introducing some variations: the doubling of the gallery above the sequence of three splayed portals, and the shortening of the arcaded transenna compressed between the two towers. The decorative elements are markedly more sumptuous, and in a sort of *horror vacui,* they cover every surface and embellish the architectural elements, forming a complex iconographic scheme.

Viollet-le-Duc, who directed the restoration work carried out from 1849 onwards, considered Amiens Cathedral the unparalleled masterpiece of Gothic architecture.

88 ■ This view of the cathedral cloister draws attention to the Bell Harry Tower, which rises some 246 ft (75 m).

88-89 ■ The aerial view of the cathedral complex highlights the different buildings that make it up: the longitudinal structure of the church, the quadrangular plan of the cloister and the buildings of the Chapter House and Library.

CHRIST'S
CATHEDRAL

[CANTERBURY ■ UNITED KINGDOM]

Canterbury Cathedral is now the seat of the Anglican Archbishop of Canterbury, who is the primate of England and the head of the Church of England. The building's role as guide to the Anglican communities is also acknowledged in its full name: Cathedral and Metropolitan Church of Christ at Canterbury. It is also included on the UNESCO World Heritage List, together with St. Augustine's Abbey and St. Martin's Church. The cathedral was founded in 597 by St. Augustine; he had been sent to England by Pope Gregory the Great and was welcomed by King Ethelbert, whose queen was already a Christian. In 1067 the

earlier building was destroyed, and in 1070 work began on the current structure over its ruins, which were recently discovered beneath the central nave in the course of archaeological investigations. Only a few elements from the Norman church – the crypt and part of the transept – survived the fire in 1174; this is why the church is considered one of the earliest examples of Gothic architecture, which derived from the influence of the Paris region. Indeed, the reconstruction of the choir with the ambulatory was carried out by the Frenchman Guillaume de Sens, who took inspiration from Laon and Notre-Dame in Paris. This work, followed by the construction of the Trinity Chapel, is testament to the fact that the Gothic style had firmly taken hold. This was the site of the golden shrine containing the relics of Thomas à Becket, the Archbishop of Canterbury whom Henry II caused to be murdered inside the cathedral; the relics were visited by huge numbers of pilgrims, but in 1538 Henry VIII had them destroyed, together with the golden casket that held them. Evidence of the pilgrims remains in the hollows in the floor and steps of the staircase, recalling the flocks of faithful who came to ask St. Thomas for help.

The Cathedral as it appears today has a longitudinal layout, and is sec-

Location	Style	Surface area	Type	Built
Canterbury (United Kingdom)	Gothic	48,437.60 ft²	Longitudinal plan	12th-15th centuries

90 ■ St. Michael's Chapel, also known as the Warriors' Chapel, houses the alabaster tomb of Lady Margaret Holland. She is portrayed between her two husbands, John Beaufort, Earl of Somerset, and the Duke of Clarence.

90-91 ■ The interior of the choir shows the results of the restoration work undertaken by William of Sens from 1174 onwards, gradually extended to the transept, and was later completed by "English" William in about 1200. The arrangement of the Trinity Chapel, which can be seen at the end of the choir, results from to the reuse of structures from the previous building, as is the variation in the height of the floor.

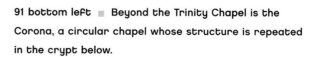

91 bottom left ■ Beyond the Trinity Chapel is the Corona, a circular chapel whose structure is repeated in the crypt below.

91 bottom right ■ The Trinity Chapel was built by "English" William to complete the choir that was begun by William of Sens: it is marked out by seven pillars, formed by coupled columns, supporting a sequence of ogival arches.

92-93 ■ Among the most celebrated elements of the
cathedral is the interior vault of the Bell Harry Tower, which
opens up at the crossing of the nave and the first transept.

tioned into three naves with rectangular bays, above which ogival rib
vaults are held up by soaring cluster pillars. A further development of
the Gothic style is seen here: the Perpendicular Style, which was the
result of the renovation ordered by Prior Thomas Chillenden in the
15th century. At the end of the nave lies the first transept, which
leads to the choir via a staircase; from here, a second transept and
another flight of steps lead to the presbytery. This culminates in the
High Altar, behind which stands the Trinity Chapel, and beyond it the
Corona, a circular chapel. The ambulatory runs along the entire area
of the presbytery; the choir stalls are separated from it by a
screen and by robust cylindrical and hexagonal columns, topped with
acanthus leaf capitals. The ogival arcades are repeated at the level
of the triforium and the clerestory, and are connected by shafts of
black Purbeck marble, which contrast with the light-colored Caen
stone used for the walls. This partition continues in the second
transept and is expanded in the Trinity Chapel. The bell tower, known

as the Bell Harry Tower, rises above the crossing of the nave and the central transept and was completed in the 16th century: indeed, the inside of lantern is covered in elaborately carved fan vaulting, contrasting with the Perpendicular Style of the vaults in the nave.

The cathedral's façade is flanked by two towers, supported by sturdy buttresses sweeping down to the ground and topped with spindly pinnacles; this structure is repeated on the sides of the church, where the tall ogival windows stand between the buttresses, supporting the aisles and rising in simple flying buttresses to support the clerestory. Annexed to the cathedral is a monastic complex, made up of the cloister, which is adjacent to the north side of the church, the chapterhouse and the library.

93 ■ The magnificent nave is an early example of the Perpendicular Style, and is thought to have been designed by Henry Yevele. It has elegant cluster pillars and rib vaults. It took around twenty-eight years to complete.

CATHEDRAL OF
ST. ANDREW

[WELLS ■ UNITED KINGDOM]

The various phases of English Gothic architecture – the Early English, the Decorated and the Perpendicular Style – are all found in Wells Cathedral, and expressed in a highly original way, making it a truly unique architectural masterpiece. Erected on the ruins of a previous Norman construction, with a cloister attached, the cathedral owes its current form to Bishop Reginald de Bohun. It is he who is thought to have had the transept, the eastern bays of the nave and the western bays of the choir built at the end of the 12th century. Much of the construction of the central nave and the façade was later completed by Bishop Jocelyn of Wells, who was keenly ambitious to create a majestic cathedral.

Indeed, the main façade has a spectacular design; the imposing frontage is developed widthways. It is 147.6 ft (45 m) wide, double the width of the nave, which it stretches across externally; on each side it has angular, square towers without pinnacles, which have robust, richly decorated buttresses. They lend verticality to the façade as a whole, while sturdy cornices divide it into three horizontal tiers; these have niches containing statues and blind arcades. Of the five

94 and 95 ■ The two imposing square towers on the main frontage of Wells Cathedral frame and complete the façade, which was designed to hold at least five hundred sculptures. Top, flanked by angels is the figure of Christ seated. Below are the statues of apostles, kings and martyrs.

96 ■ The Chapter
House has an octagonal
plan, arranged around
an elegant central
pillar, from which thirty-
two ribs spring out.
These in turn are
connected in the vaults
with ribs radiating out
from the eight half-
columns placed around
the perimeter of the
room.

97 ■ The sequence of
ogival arches which
defines the central
nave ends in the
brilliant static
solution of the
"inverted arches" at
the crossing, which
were designed to hold
the weight of the
central tower above it.

hundred sculptures that originally decorated the niches – many of which are human-sized – just over three hundred have survived. Between 1974 and 1986 during the cleaning and conservation of the masonry frontage, it was found that the statues had traces of color; it therefore became clear that they would have stood out in dramatic contrast against the pale stonework.

The entrance to the church is through the main façade. The interior consists of the usual Latin-cross floor plan with a three-aisled nave with the transept at the midpoint; beyond the transept is the rectangular choir and the apse, which was originally square but was later replaced by a polygonal apse.

The nave is divided into rectangular bays by a regular sequence of cluster pillars with pointed arches above. A plain cornice separates these arches from the triforium; the latter is a markedly horizontal band into which plunge the ribs of the vaults which divide the clerestory.

Indeed, Gothic verticalism is reconciled here with local tradition, making the nave a remarkable example of the Early English style. Particularly interesting is the introduction of the striking "scissor arches" that help the crossing to hold the weight of the central tower; the latter was completed during the time of the Perpendicular Style, and is embellished with slim pinnacles. The inverted arches are stacked against each other, joined at the top and open at floor level and at the impost of the vault. They provided a visible termination for the main nave and the transept, and radically renewed the church's interior appearance. Beyond the crossing, the choir vaulting, the vaults in the Lady Chapel corresponding to the polygonal apse and those in the Chapter House bear all the hallmarks of the Decorated Style. They are formed by a tight network of narrow ribs, whereby ribs with no structural function are used for purely decorative purposes; especially in the Chapter House, where the ribs of the eight pillars placed at each corner of the octagon come together in the vault, and are gathered in a fan shape by the room's single central pillar. The Chapter House, together with the cloister and the vicar's residence, was built upon the cathedral's completion between the 13th and 15th centuries.

Location	Style	Surface area	Type	Built
Wells (United Kingdom)	Gothic	40,687.58 ft²	Longitudinal plan	12th-15th centuries

CATHEDRAL OF
OUR LADY

[BURGOS ■ SPAIN]

Burgos Cathedral is the oldest of Spain's large Gothic cathedrals. The first stone was laid on 20 July 1221, in the presence of the King of Castile, Ferdinand III, and Bishop Mauricio. Work on the cathedral continued swiftly until the façade was completed in the second half of the 13th century. Over the three centuries that followed the cathedral took on its current appearance, with the construction of the side chapels, the spires on the towers on the façade, the Chapel of the Condestable (1492-1532) and the crossing tower of the *cimborrio* (1540-1578).

The cathedral's location in the heart of the old town center is extremely picturesque, as it towers over a rocky base. The imposing mass of the cathedral has large expanses of masonry that recall Romanesque architecture; the building is rendered lighter by the pale color of the limestone – *piedra de Hontoria de la Cantera* – and by its pinnacles and traceried spires in the Gothic style.

The architects of Burgos Cathedral took their inspiration – making adjustments based on the local Hispano-Moorish tradition – from the great French and English cathedrals of the 13th century. From the former, they took the floor plan, the division of the nave elevation into three tiers, the composition of the

98 ■ **The Cathedral of Santa Maria towers over the town of Burgos. Seen here, from left to right are the two impressive towers of the façade and the spires that rise above the projecting structures of the crossing and the main chapel at the head of the chevet.**

99 ■ **The two traceried spires on the façade above the Gothic towers were commissioned by Bishop Alonso of Cartagena and were built between by Juan de Colonia between 1442-1458. Burgos Cathedral is the only Spanish Gothic cathedral to have been declared a UNESCO World Heritage Site.**

façade with towers at either side; while English architecture's typical taste for complicated interwoven ribbing immediately became popular in Spain, as it tied in with the tradition of decorative ribbing found in Arab architecture.

The cathedral has a three-aisled nave with a projecting transept, a deep presbytery and ambulatory which originally opened into five radiating chapels. Over the course of four centuries, other architectural and decorative structures were gradually layered over this simple, linear floor plan; this enriched the cathedral's internal space, and eventually created a highly original blend between Gothic and Renaissance elements. Also noteworthy are the sculpted decorations, chandeliers, screens, liturgical furnishings and tombs that, in a sort of *horror vacui*, gradually filled the space; the intelligibility of the architectural layout suffered as a result. A perfect example is the 16th-century *trascoro* or liturgical choir: it is closed off by tall screens (typically found in many Spanish cathedrals) and extends so far that it occupies half of the nave.

The work carried out during the Renaissance did however develop styles and forms that were still linked to the Gothic tradition. The most interesting of these are the chapel at the top of the ambulatory dedicated to the Purification of the Virgin – commissioned by the Condestable Fernandez de Velasco and executed by Simon de Colonia; and the reconstruction of the *cimborrio* lantern (1540-68) at the crossing of the nave and transept.

These buildings have elegant "star-burst" ribbed ceilings on the interior; while on the outside they dominate the landscape with sculpture groups of traceried spires. Two more spires formed like slender traceried pyramids airily emphasise the verticality of the façade.

100 top ■ This interior view of the cathedral shows the impost arches at the crossing and the large rose window in the south transept.

100 bottom ■ The Chapel of the Condestable has an elegant ribbed ceiling with a star-shaped central motif.

101 and 102-103 ■ The magnificent ceiling of the octagonal crossing stands at the intersection between the central nave and the transept.

Location	Style	Surface area	Type	Built
Burgos (Spain)	Gothic-Renaissance	81,805.72 ft²	Longitudinal plan	13th-16th centuries

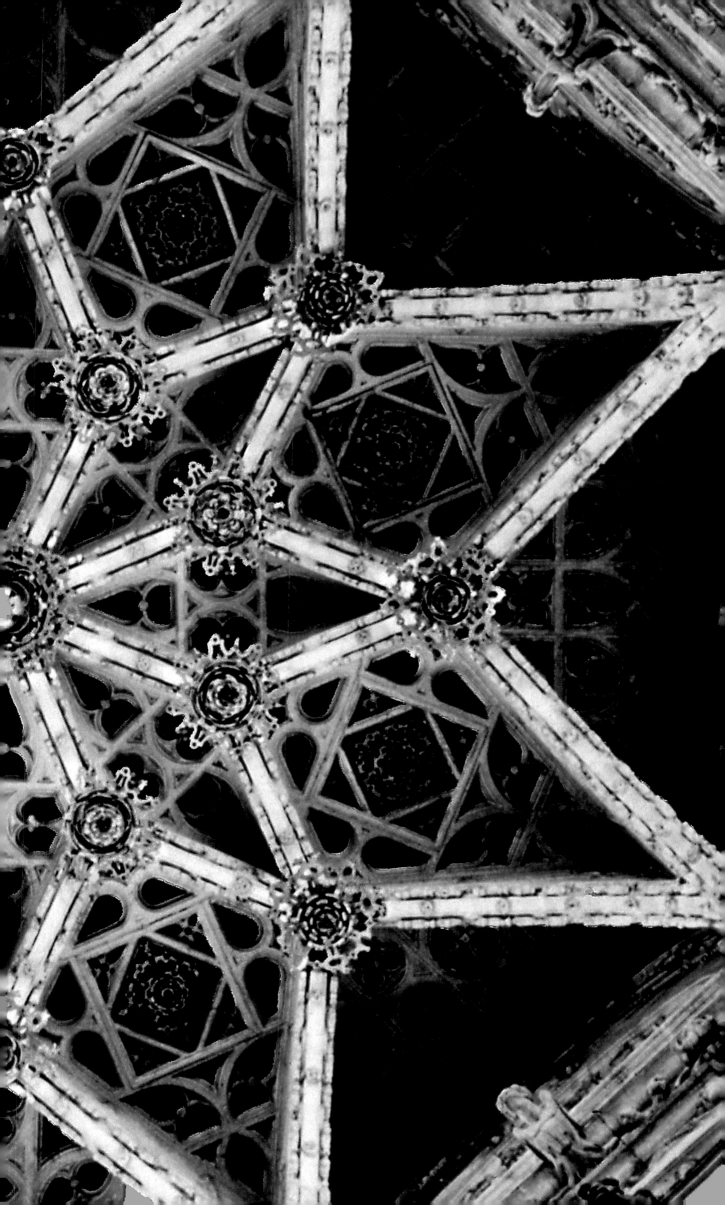

CATHEDRAL OF
ST. PETER

[REGENSBURG ▪ GERMANY]

Regensburg Cathedral is considered the most important Gothic building in Bavaria. It was built to replace the previous Carolingian-Ottonian construction, the position and dimensions of which it retains, while updating its architectural appearance.

Initially, only the atrium and transept at the entrance of the old cathedral were demolished; the main longitudinal body was retained to allow services to continue as usual. One of the towers of the transept was also kept as an extra bell tower from the new building, since work on it was proceeding so slowly, starting from the choir. Known as the Donkey Tower, it is now part of the side of the cathedral which is separated from the Carolingian cloister which was originally attached to the building. Little documentation regarding this construction work has survived. All that is certain is that the work was already underway in 1266, during the episcopate of Bishop Leo Thundorfer. In 1325 the

104 ▪ The twin 344.5 ft (105 m) towers dominate the façade. Begun later than the cathedral, they were finally completed by Franz Denzingen in the 19th century.

105 ▪ This view from the top of the cathedral shows the length of the longitudinal body, from the soaring towers on the façade to the series of buttresses, flying buttresses and pinnacles on the side and the transept, as far as the apse.

106 ■ This detail of the stained glass window depicts a Maestà framed by three columns, topped with ornately decorated arches. It illustrates the Adoration of the Magi.

107 ■ The ogival rib vaults of the nave conclude in the sunburst of ribbed vaults over the apse, which has a double order of large windows.

apse, choir, transept and the first bay of the main nave were completed. At this point, part of the surrounding building had to be demolished, as well as the existing church of St. John, in order to continue building the nave in a westerly direction. In around 1470, the main nave of the church, part of the façade and several stories of the surrounding towers had been completed, although some bays were still missing from the roof. In the meantime, the community's financial resources also dwindled as Regensburg's status as a trade center declined.

Lastly, disagreements between the emperor and the citizens became increasingly serious and in this difficult situation, the director of the cathedral building yard, the master builder Wolfgang Roritzer, was beheaded. Nevertheless, in 1525 the third storey of the towers was completed; then, after the Protestant Reformation had taken hold, the building work came to an abrupt stop. It was only in the first half of the 17th century thanks to Bishop Albert IV von Törring that the last three bays of the church were covered and the Baroque altars were introduced. In the 19th century restoration work carried out by the architect Friedrich von Gärtner removed the 17th century elements from the interior, except for the High Altar; Francesco Detzinger then built the last level of the towers and the pediment of the transept. After about six centuries, the building work was finally finished.

Regensburg Cathedral as it is today consists of a Latin-cross floor plan with a three-aisled nave (280 ft/85.4 m long, 114 ft/34.8 m wide); it has a non-projecting transept followed by a short choir and a polygonal apse. The southern side of the church has a series of coupled windows which alternate with sturdy buttresses, above which are airy flying buttresses topped with intricately sculpted gargoyles, spires and pinnacles. This structural geometry is repeated in the choir and the polygonal end of the apse; the apse is pierced by a double order of windows which, from the inside, seem to create a continuous glazed surface. The cluster pillars in the nave and aisles bring the ribbing of the large ogival vaults down to floor level; meanwhile, between the arcades that link the pillars and the vaults there is the flat gallery of the triforium. The interior is particularly rich in decorations, stained glass dating from the 13th and 14th centuries and unusual sculpture groups; for example, the depiction of the Devil and the Devil's grandmother – with an animal's body and human face – placed in two niches in the front wall of the nave.

Location	Style	Surface area	Type	Built
REGENSBURG (GERMANY)	GOTHIC	31,990.34 FT²	LONGITUDINAL PLAN	13TH-17TH CENTURIES

CATHEDRAL OF
SANTA MARIA ASSUNTA

[ORVIETO ■ ITALY]

Construction began on the new cathedral of Orvieto in 1290, by order of Bishop Francesco Monaldeschi. Interpreting the wishes of the townspeople, he decided to demolish the old, dilapidated 12th-century cathedral of Santa Maria del Vescovado and the nearby parish church of San Costanzo, in order to clear an area that would be sufficiently large for the task. Indeed, the new building was to be an expression of the civil and economic ascent of the city of Orvieto; the Commune did its part by launching a specific tax-collection campaign.

The choice of a basilica-style layout – which was also used elsewhere such as in the Basilica of Assisi, the Cathedral of Siena and the church of Santa Maria Novella in Florence –

108 and 108-109 ■ The façade of Orvieto Cathedral is known for its severe architectural lines: the detail of the upper part, which was built in the 14th century, shows the rose window with the head of the Redeemer in the center. The cornice around the window has niches containing fifty-two heads in relief. Top, a detail of the sumptuous decoration above one of the three portals.

Façade postérieure de la Cathédrale : 1 : 100.

reflects the difficulty that the new spatial canons of Gothic art had in gaining ground in a country like Italy, which was influenced by a strong Early Christian and Romanic tradition. In Orvieto Cathedral, the Latin cross layout has three naves with semi-circular side chapels, a protruding transept and a square apse; the naves in the longitudinal section have traditional wooden truss ceilings (fitted at different heights), while only the transept and the apse have cross-vaulted ceilings.

The same Early Christian-inspired taste is also apparent in the elevation of the central nave, which is defined by a sequence of massive circular-section pillars supporting round arches; these are topped by a horizontal gallery, with tall windows above it. The interior features horizontal striped black and white marble facing on all the surfaces, including the pillars and the archivolts. This bi-chromatic effect is typical of the Tuscan Romanic style; it is also found on the exterior, on the side façades, which are defined by the shape of the naves and the sequence of convex chapels. The façade is considered one of the masterpieces of Italian Gothic architecture: it was begun in 1310 by the Sienese Lorenzo Maitani, and completed

Location	Style	Surface area	Type	Built
Orvieto (Italy)	Gothic	31,849.60 ft²	Latin-cross plan	13th-14th centuries

110 ■ In this drawing from 1834, Robert Ruprich focuses on the façade on the rear of the cathedral: in the foreground is the large Gothic four-light window that lights the apse.

110-111 ■ This aerial view highlights the sheer size of the cathedral, which dominates the old center of Orvieto.

111 bottom ■ In the foreground of this drawing of the side of the cathedral, Robert Ruprich shows the cylindrical-shaped chapels projecting outwards from the main structure of the side aisle.

→ →

112 ■ This view of the main nave shows the apsidal area in the background, decorated with the vast painted cycle of the Stories of the Virgin Mary.

113 ■ This picture shows the crossing between the main nave, with its wooden Truss ceiling, and the transept, with cross vault ceiling.

114-115 ■ The chapel of San Brizio was built between 1406-1425 at the southern end of the transept. It contains a major fresco cycle that was the work of two leading painters of the Italian Renaissance, Beato Angelico (late 15th century) and Luca Signorelli (early 16th century).

over the next three centuries. Artists and architects of the caliber of Andrea Pisano, Michele Sanmicheli and Antonio da Sangallo il Giovane each made their contribution. Its architecture features a clear geometrical layout, divided into three vertical sections and arranged over three levels horizontally. It includes elements that are also found in Northern European cathedrals (the side towers, the pinnacles, the central rose window, the arched gallery, the splayed portals); here, however, they are interpreted with a different artistic and spatial sensibility. As a result, the sculptural modeling of the façade is more restrained and the decorative elements are more measured, and always subordinate to the clarity of the architectural layout. Furthermore, the importance given to the wall – an element which is typical of the Italian Gothic – is reflected in the decoration of large surfaces with mosaics on gold backgrounds, which enrich the façade with evocative effects of color, blending into a perfect expressive union with the stained glass windows and sculptural elements.

from the RENAISSANCE to HISTORICISM

This section looks at various periods in the history of architecture: from the birth of the Renaissance in 15th-century Italy, to its spread first through Europe and then across the rest of the world, up to the Neo-Classical age

(18th century), then culminating in 19th-century historicism. What the Renaissance, the Baroque, Neo-Classical and the stylistic revivals of the 19th century all have in common is their references to the architecture of previous centuries: Greco-Roman classicism or the Gothic, Romanesque and Byzantine styles, since we are referring here to religious architecture. Naturally, that is a simplified statement as each of these various revivals of earlier architecture came about for specific reasons and purposes.

The term "Renaissance" alludes to the desire to give a rebirth to classical antiquity. It was not merely a banal imitation of formal solutions, types or spatial organisms; rather, it was an imitation of the use of the syntactical and grammatical language of ancient architecture, based on certain architectural dictates. The result was a totally new kind of architecture, which would even be capable of surpassing its model of inspiration. In order to achieve this, Filippo Brunelleschi (1377-1446) blended the rebirth of the classical language with the perfection of a new vision of

perspective; he thus fulfilled the principles of regularity, symmetry and proportion. The benchmark text for all concerned was the *De Architectura* by Vitruvius (a Roman architect who lived in the 1st century A.D.). This is the only surviving treatise from antiquity which was reprised, reinterpreted and illustrated by leading theorists from the Renaissance onwards.

With regard to religious architecture specifically, all Renaissance treatises favored the centralized plan, combining the geometrical perfection of the central plan with the perfection of God, who created the world according to the laws of mathematics: the church is therefore interpreted not as *ecclesia* (from the Latin for "assembly"), but as *templum* (from the Latin for "house of God"). In practice, this theoretical approach clashed with the inclinations of the ecclesiastical hierarchies. For liturgical reasons, they preferred Latin-cross (longitudinal) plan churches, especially for large buildings such as basilicas and cathedrals. All of Renaissance religious architecture was influenced by the question of the use of the central plan rather than

From top to bottom: Basilica of Sant'Andrea, Mantova, Italy; Basilica of Santa Maria delle Grazie, Milan, Italy; Basilica of Santa Maria della Salute, Venice, Italy; Chiesa di Sant'Ivo della Sapienza, Rome, Italy; Church of St. Charles Borromeo, Vienna, Austria; Church of Sainte Geneviève (Panthéon), Paris, France; Cathedral of Sainte-Marie-Majeure, Marseilles, France; Paul Abadie (1812-1884), Projet pour l'église du Sacré-Coeur, coupe transversale, 1874.

the longitudinal plan; this reached its apex when St. Peter's Basilica was built in Rome. This building confirmed the supremacy of the more usual longitudinal plan, although it was strongly marked by a large centralized space beneath the dome. This solution was also adopted for Granada cathedral, where the longitudinal body of the nave and aisles ends in a chevet with a majestic semi-circular domed space. Above all, it was during the Baroque period that architects devised mixed layouts with centralized Latin cross plans or elongated central plans. An interesting example of this variety is the basilica of the Vierzehnheiligen. Within a longitudinal plan, it contains three elliptical spatial units with structures that stand apart from the outside walls.

Neo-Classicism developed as a reaction against what were considered to be the excesses of the Baroque and Rococo styles. It reclaimed the ancient structural significance of architectural orders, combining this with the quest for a "national spirit." In the church of Sainte-Geneviève in Paris, Jacques-Germain Soufflot (1713-80) aimed to blend the purity of Greek architectural forms (discovered thanks to archaeological digs in Greece and southern Italy) with the lightness of the Gothic structure, which was considered an authentically French style.

Another time at which ancient architecture was reprised was during the stylistic revivals in the 19th century. Then, the past was considered as a treasure trove of forms that could be dipped into at will; an emblematic example is Marseilles Cathedral, designed by Léon Vaudoyer (1803-72). It contains a combination of Neo-Byzantine and Neo-Romanesque forms, with the aim of alluding to the harbor city's ongoing cultural exchanges.

SANTA MARIA DEL FIORE

[FLORENCE ■ ITALY]

The Cathedral or Duomo of Santa Maria del Fiore is one of the most famous monumental complexes in western architecture. It is located in the old center of Florence; standing separately to the right of the façade is the bell tower started by Giotto in 1334 (completed by Andrea Pisano and finished by Francesco Talenti in 1359), while opposite stands the old 11th-century Romanesque baptistery.

The current appearance of the Cathedral of Santa Maria del Fiore is the result of a gradual layering of various demolition, reconstruction and enlargement projects carried out over a period spanning six centuries. The Latin-cross floor plan was begun by Arnolfo di Cambio starting in 1296, and expanded after 1396 by Francesco Talenti. He retained the original shape of the octagonal chevet with pentagonal lobes, but made it so large that, at that time, it was quite impossible to build the roof. Only Filippo Brunelleschi, the undisputed master of the early Italian Renaissance, was able to manage it. Between 1420 and 1436 he accomplished

118 ■ Santa Maria del Fiore has a three-aisled basilica plan; this is followed in the chevet by a centralized part, with an octagon from which three pentagonal lobes project outwards. Each of the three lobes contains five square chapels.

119 ■ The mass of the dome, surrounded by the lobes of the chapels with galleries above them, was a foretaste of that typically Renaissance interest in central-plan structures.

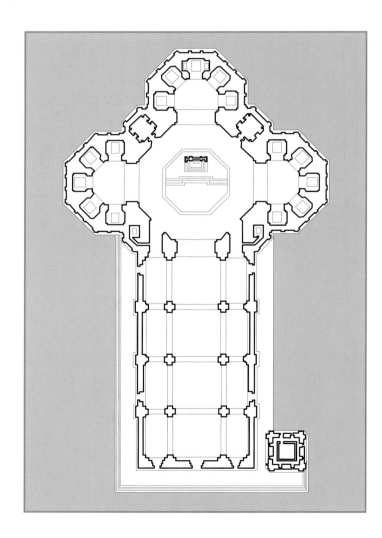

the task of creating a dome to cover the large octagonal space with a diameter of some 141 ft (43 m).

The building was then finished by Emilio De Fabris in the second half of the 19th century, when he created the façade in keeping with and inspired by Arnolfo di Cambio's original design.

Brunelleschi's ingenious idea was to use various construction techniques that the ancient Romans used to cover the large vaulted buildings of the imperial age (such as the dome of the Pantheon in Rome). He did, however, adapt these methods to the octagonal layout which, compared to a circular one, presents greater structural problems due to the unequal distribution of stress. He therefore used a rotated dome – with beds of bricks placed on surfaces that were not horizontal but conical; he built it using a sequence of masonry rings, guaranteeing the dome's stability through the "herringbone" arrangement of

120-121 ■ This image shows the "swollen" ogival profile of the dome, held between stone ribs and topped with the lantern. The octagonal drum with its oculus windows raised the dome much higher than the roof of the nave.

Location	Style	Surface area	Type	Built
FLORENCE (ITALY)	GOTHIC-RENAISSANCE-NEO-GOTHIC	73,194.59 FT²	LONGITUDINAL PLAN	13TH-15TH CENTURIES

121 top ■ The lantern above the dome was designed by Brunelleschi. It has elegant buttresses that echo the arrangement of the ribs on the dome.

121 bottom ■ These two drawings show a cross section of the dome, highlighting the two shells built one over the other.

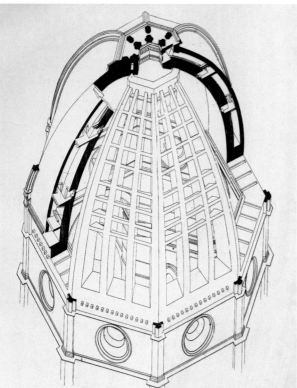

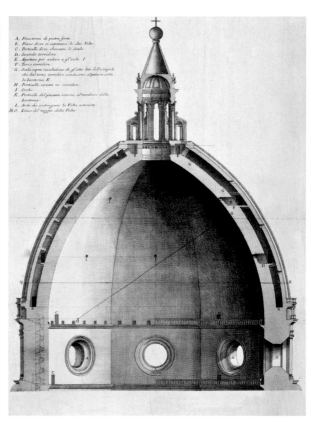

the bricks. The rows of bricks were alternated with elements placed vertically – on edge – to prevent them from slipping, so that it was possible to build the dome gradually without using a supporting framework. Then, to reduce lateral thrust to a minimum, at the angles of the octagon he inserted stone ribs with pointed profiles (the pointed arch exerts less lateral thrust than a round arch), thus making the old late-Gothic techniques work to his advantage. He also decided to create a double shell with an inner space so as to render the structure lighter, protect the inner dome from humidity and to be able to inspect it. Each of the two domes has a different shape: the inner shell

is vaulted with a pointed fifth curvature (as provided for by the specifications for the Cathedral project) while the external one is vaulted with a pointed fourth curvature, giving it its characteristic pointed "swollen" shape.

With this work, Filippo Brunelleschi demonstrated his incredible skills as a master builder and architect. He completed a building from another era, totally redefining its significance without betraying the spirit of the late-Gothic construction.

The dome of Santa Maria del Fiore very soon came to symbolize the power of Florence over all the Tuscan peoples – *"structura si grande, erta sopra e cieli, ampla da coprire chon sua ombra tutti e popoli toscani..."* ("Such a large structure, rising above the skies, ample to cover with its shadow all of the Tuscan people. . . "; Leon Battista Alberti, *De Pictura*, 1436) – and its great success meant that the architectural element of the dome became one of the key themes of the entire Renaissance.

122-123 ■ The picture shows a detail of the marble facing on the façade, embellished with statues and bas-reliefs.

123 top ■ The façade begun by Arnolfo di Cambio was never completed and was demolished in 1586. It was completely reworked in neo-Gothic style by Emilio De Fabris in 1867-1887.

123 bottom ■ The picture shows the bas-relief on the pinnacle above the central portal.

124 ■ A view from above of the central nave highlights the polychrome marble floor.

124-125 ■ The longitudinal section of the cathedral was built in the 13th century and is a single, uninterrupted space, simply marked out with the pillars in the central nave.

125 bottom ■ Contrary to Brunelleschi's intention that it remained a purely architectural element, the surface of the dome, measuring over 4000 square meters, was frescoed by Giorgio Vasari starting in 1572. He divided the space into six concentric registers one above the other. The work was completed in 1579 by Federico Zuccari.

SAN LORENZO

[FLORENCE ■ ITALY]

The famous monumental complex of San Lorenzo is situated in the old town center of Florence. It includes the monastery, with the Biblioteca Laurenziana by Michelangelo Buonarroti (1524-59); the basilica designed by Filippo Brunelleschi, with its two splendid sacristies – one the Sacrestia Vecchia (Old Sacristy) by Brunelleschi himself, the other the Sacrestia Nuova (New Sacristy) by Michelangelo (1520-34); and the 17th-century Cappella dei Principi (Princes' Chapel) which was added at the top of the chevet.

The Basilica of San Lorenzo was rebuilt by the Medici family, starting in 1423. It was one of the greatest achievements of Filippo Brunelleschi, and of the Italian Renaissance as a whole. Indeed, it can be said that with this work, the great Florentine architect "invented" the Renaissance: he used the syntactic and grammatical language of classical architecture and inserted it into a new concept of space, based on the discovery of the rules of perspective.

The basilica has a Latin-cross floor plan which has a three-aisled nave with side chapels, a transept and a square apse flanked by two chapels either side, and by the two famous sacristies, which use the same theme of the central floor-plan to produce different results. The

126 ■ This aerial view highlights the octagonal shape of the imposing funeral chapel of the Medici family. It was built starting in 1604, at the end of the chevet of the Basilica of San Lorenzo.

127 ■ In the main nave, the classical Corinthian columns are topped with a so-called "Brunelleschi dado": this is a sort of shortened trabeation, with a sequence of round arches above it.

dome on pendentives stands above the crossing of the nave and transept. It was completed by Duccio Manetti following Brunelleschi's death. The façade was never completed.

The regularity of the floor plan is the result of a modular design, based on the repetition of two fundamental measurements: the spacing of the lower order – defined by the sequence of colonnades – establishes the sides of the square bays of the side-aisles; the distance between the pilaster strips in the upper order which frame the space within the dome, determines the width of the central nave and the transept. Applying the same principle vertically, it is the height of the two orders which determines the heights of the various roofs: a flat lacunar ceiling for the central nave and the transept, ribbed vaults in the side-aisles and barrel vaults in the side chapels. The elevations of the central nave pick up on the scheme Brunelleschi had already used in the portico of the Innocenti, developing it into a bilateral symmetry. A sequence of round arches is supported by classic Corinthian columns; tangent to the archivolts runs the trabeation of the upper order of angular pilaster strips (the two orders are linked together); the flat wall above is interspersed with

Location	Style	Surface area	Type	Built
FLORENCE (ITALY)	RENAISSANCE	38,211.88 FT²	LONGITUDINAL PLAN	15TH-17TH CENTURIES

single-light windows which are aligned with the archivolts. Projecting the system of arches on columns onto the back wall of the side-aisles results in a series of pilaster strips supporting a continuous trabeation that runs tangent to the arched entrances to the chapels. Brunelleschi took inspiration from the elevation typically found in Romanesque churches. He standardized the individual architectural elements with a logic of perfect perspective, and also used a rigorous Corinthian order which he drew directly from Roman antiquities. The lacunar ceiling also derives from Roman basilicas.

Unlike medieval buildings, which are complex palimpsests of architecture, sculpture and painting, in the Basilica of San Lorenzo the construction of the inner space is dictated purely by the architecture. The grey stone known as *pietra serena* used for the framework (archivolts, trabeations, columns, pilaster strips) defines a rigorous structure of perspective which contrasts against the whiteness of the stucco walls, creating an evocative effect of peace and serenity in worshippers and visitors.

128-129 ■ This view of the Sacrestia Nuova by Michelangelo Buonarroti shows the sculpture group on the tomb of Lorenzo de' Medici, with the two allegorical figures of Dawn and Dusk.

129 ■ Brunelleschi's Sacrestia Vecchia consists of two square plan rooms with domed ceilings.

ST. PETER'S

BASILICA

[VATICAN STATE]

St. Peter's Basilica in the Vatican, built upon the burial place of the apostle Peter, is the largest and most important church in Christendom. The events leading up to its construction were highly complex and arduous. According to reports, they began on 18 April 1506 when demolition of the earlier Constantinian basilica began, and finished over 150 years later, in the second half of the 17 century with the construction of the large Baroque square. The idea of renovating the ancient, glorious Early Christian basilica, built between 315 and 349,

130-131 and 131 ■ These two aerial views show the architectural complex of St. Peter's Basilica from two points opposite the Via della Conciliazione, which was opened in 1940 to create a monumental axis leading to the basilica.

came as early as 1452 when Pope Nicholas V (1447-1455), following advice from Leon Battista Alberti, commissioned Bernardo Rossellino to expand the apsidal area. The structural justifications for this – some of the brickwork was dangerously unaligned – actually hid the real intention of bringing the basilica's architecture up to date with the new Renaissance taste. However, it was Pope Julius II (1503-1513) who took up this idea with renewed vigor. He commissioned the most celebrated architect of the time, Donato Bramante, to totally rebuild the basilica, which was also to hold the Pope's tomb, a vast monument that Michelangelo Buonarroti was already working on. It was probably also due to this – as mausoleums usually have a centralized plan – that Bramante chose a central plan consisting of an apsed Greek cross inscribed within a square and topped by a vast dome similar to that of the Pantheon. Four smaller domes were planned for the sides of the cross, to cover other centralized spaces that repeated the cross plan on a smaller scale. The project also included raising the four bell

132 ■ The plans by Donato Bramante (left) and Carlo Maderno (right) show how the design evolved from Bramante's original idea to the final solution, based on inserting a three-aisled longitudinal body into the centralised plan built by Michelangelo.

133 ■ The main nave has three arcades on thick pillars with Corinthian pilaster strips against them. They support the barrel vault, decorated with a gilded stucco coffered ceiling. The walls are entirely covered in marbles, stuccos and mosaics.

towers at the corners of the square; however, all that was actually carried out was the massive piers at the crossing and the large arch imposts of the dome. After Bramante's death, various architects took over, from Raffaello to Baldassarre Peruzzi and Antonio da San Gallo il Giovane. They gradually departed from Bramante's vision, also suggesting Latin-cross plans. This intense reworking of the design, which had a strong impact on architectural culture in those years (and in the years to come), reflects the typically Renaissance debate between the use of the central plan rather than the Latin-cross plan. The superiority of the central plan derived from the preference, confirmed by all the architectural treatises of the time (from Francesco di Giorgio Martini, to Filarete and Leon Battista Alberti), for the elementary geometrical forms that were closest to the principles of clarity and rationality that Renaissance culture celebrated. In this sense, the Greek cross inscribed in the square, which Bramante suggested for St. Peter's, united the aspiration to centrality which symbolically represented the universe covered by the celestial vault, and the Christian symbolism of Christ's cross with the tomb of the apostle Peter at its center. In 1546 Pope Paul III (1543-1549) appointed Michelangelo, at the age of 72, as head architect of the building site, the Fabbrica di San Pietro. He also authorized him, through the device of *motu proprio* (on your own motion), to take any decisions on the matter. Michelangelo then proceeded to demolish much of the building erected by San Gallo, as he found it too heavy, dark and overloaded with different elements. He then proposed a new Greek-cross plan, with the aim of restoring the spirit of Bramante's project. He did however partly modify Bramante's design by creating a more organic, united form, dominated by the vast space of the central dome.

LOCATION	STYLE	SURFACE AREA	TYPE	BUILT
ROME (VATICAN)	RENAISSANCE-BAROQUE	215,999.39 FT²	LONGITUDINAL PLAN	16TH-17TH CENTURIES

When he died in 1564, the building was almost complete, apart from the dome and the façade. They were completed by Giacomo della Porta (1572) and Carlo Maderno (1607-1614) respectively. The latter fulfilled the wishes of Pope Paul V (1605-1621) by lengthening Michelangelo's construction by as many as three bays, thus turning it into the current Latin-cross plan. The final dimensions of the construction as a whole are vast. The inside surface area is over 215,000 sq. ft (20,000 sq. m), and can hold 60,000 people. The building's size is, however, skillfully played down by the perfect harmony of proportions between the individual architectural elements.

The third major figure in the construction of St. Peter's was undoubtedly Gian Lorenzo Bernini. He directed the work to decorate the interior of the basilica (from 1629), and created the stunning architecture of the bronze baldacchino above the papal altar (1624-1633) and the majestic St. Peter's Throne in the apse (1656-1665). Bernini was also given the task of designing the square in front of the basilica. He managed this by carefully

fitting the basilica into the existing streets around it: a spectacular elliptical plaza circled by two

quadruple rows of 280 columns, over 49.2 ft (15 m) tall, are linked to the façade via two straight corridors, creating an additional pentagonal square. The form and size of this square were designed to counterbalance Maderno's over-powering façade and emphasize Michelangelo's dome. Bernini also gave the shape of the square a symbolic meaning: *"to maternally welcome with open arms Catholics to confirm them in their faith, heretics to bring them back to the Church, and infidels to show them the light of true faith."* (Bernini)

134-135 ◼ The baldacchino, designed by Bernini and Borromini, is a vast bronze structure, ca. 98.4 ft (30 m) in height.

135 ◼ For the Throne of St. Peter, Bernini inserted the ancient wooden chair used by the apostle Peter into a majestic throne, supported by statues of Holy Doctors of the church.

136-137 ◼ The mosaic decorations in the dome are by Cavalier d'Arpino (1602-1612). They depict Christ, the apostles and busts of popes and saints.

BASILICA OF
GESÙ CRISTO REDENTORE

[VENICE ■ ITALY]

In order to fulfill a vow made during the 1575-76 plague, the Senate of Venice decided to build the church of the Redentore on Giudecca Island. It assigned the project to Andrea Palladio. After the famous architect's death in 1580, the work was finished by the foreman Antonio da Ponte, and the church was consecrated in 1592. Even today, each year on the third Sunday in July, the faithful cross the Giudecca canal over a makeshift bridge of boats, to give thanks to the Redeemer. Palladio's architectural layout is an exemplary blend of the central plan – which was that preferred by Italian Renaissance architects (from Brunelleschi to Bramante and Michelangelo) – and the Latin-cross plan, which was favored by the ecclesiastical hierarchy for practical reasons linked to the performance of the liturgy. In fact, the basilica has three separate areas, although they are connected to each other: a vast central nave, bordered by pillar arcades which enclose the side chapels – three on each side, interconnected so as to form side aisles – is covered by a barrel vault with large thermal windows; a large central space – the so-called tribune – defined on two sides by

138 ■ Ottavio Bertotti Scamozzi's 18th century drawing highlights the rigorous architectural layout of the façade of the Redentore.

139 top ■ The design of the façade is based on a repetition of the shape of the pediment found on classical temples.

139 bottom ■ The drawing of the floor plan is by Francesco Muttoni (1740-48), while the longitudinal section is by Ottavio Bertotti Scamozzi (1776-82): note the large area of the dome-vaulted tribune that towers above the chevet.

140 ■ This photograph shows the dome on pendentives that rises above the tribune. It is supported by large angular pillars with half-columns against them.

semi-circular apses and on the third side, where the choir is, by a transenna of columns (exedra), is vaulted with an elegant dome on a drum; while the choir, situated in a deep chapel with a semi-circular termination, is flanked by two quadrangular chapels, one of which functions as a sacristy. The passage between the central nave and the tribune is achieved through a slight narrowing of the nave, which is emphasized by half-columns leaning against the pillars, and by a triumphal arch. Another triumphal arch above the exedra separates the choir from the presbytery. The inner space of the church is marked out by the Corinthian columns and half-columns which support a continuous trabeation which runs around the spaces of the nave and the tribune (including the exedra), connecting them together. The columns, half-columns and pilaster-strips are made from brickwork (except for the sculpted parts, which are in stone). Their surfaces, as with those of the walls and vaults, are plastered with white stucco; this causes a modulation of the effects of refracted light, with a painterly sensibility that is typical of the Venetian school. Inside, the classical references are taken from Imperial Roman architecture – the concept of the wall as a plastic structural mass, the use of thermal windows and the screens of columns; on the exterior, however, the theme of the façade employs the motif of the pronaos of the classical temple projected onto the plane: on a larger scale in the central area, and on a smaller scale, divided in two, in the side areas. Palladio thus managed to evoke the church's interior space (divided into a central nave and side chapels) in a way that he had already tried out in San Francesco della Vigna and San Giorgio Maggiore. In the Redentore, a monumental staircase leads up to the façade; the façade itself is dominated by the dome and flanked by two bell towers, almost giving the impression – especially from an axial view – that the church has a central plan. This architecture expresses Palladio's extraordinary skill in mingling Venetian tradition – the dome is Byzantine-derived, the buttresses supporting the nave are typically Gothic – with the new Renaissance culture. He expressed the latter through his use of architectural elements derived from Roman antiquities, and by using a humanistic-style proportional system.

141 top ■ This photograph of the tribune highlights the polychrome floor decoration in typical Venetian marble.

141 bottom ■ The interior view of the main nave highlights the remarkable architectural features of the walls: surprisingly, they have no decoration at all.

Location	Style	Surface area	Type	Built
Venice (Italy)	Renaissance	18,083.37 ft²	Longitudinal plan	16th century

SANTA MARÍA
DE LA ENCARNAINCIÓN

[GRANADA ■ SPAIN]

Granada Cathedral was built starting in 1528, to a design by Diego de Siloe. It was not completed until 1703. King Charles V wanted to build a grandiose structure fitting to stand alongside the splendid *Capilla Real*, which had been built in the Gothic style by Enrique de Egas between 1506-21 to house the remains of the monarchs Ferdinand of Aragon and Isabella of Castile. The same architect was also responsible for the planimetric layout of the cathedral's foundations, built in 1523; that was before the job was assigned to the more up-to-date Diego de Siloe. He was a champion of the Renaissance style, also known as *a lo romano*, and was responsible for it being introduced to Granada. The origins of the building's architecture are therefore complex, as it blends a plan derived from Spanish Gothic designs with the new Renaissance sensibility.

The cathedral has five naves differing in height. They are flanked by deep side chapels which continue through the presbytery beyond the main transept. The latter is positioned alongside the entrance to the *Capilla Real*, which existed already. The space in the presbytery is arranged in a fairly complex way. The chapels and ambulatory, which corresponds to the second side-aisles, surround the main altar, which is the solid fulcrum of the church's architectural composition. The altar is enclosed by eight pilasters in a radial arrangement, which conclude the sequence of bays in the first side-aisles. The altar stands in a majestic circular space 72 ft (22 m) in diameter topped with a dome 147.6 ft (45 m) high and is known as the *Capilla Mayor*. Its planimetric layout recalls the Early Christian rotunda in the church of the Holy Sepulcher in Jerusalem. In fact, this rotunda was built with the intention of housing the Most Holy Sacrament as an act of reparation for Granada's Moorish past. It is no coincidence that the cathedral itself was built on a site previously occupied by a mosque. The *Capilla Mayor* provides the ideal conclusion to the central nave and is the focal point of the internal perspective view of the cathedral. However, the choir stalls were added in 1926-29, interrupting the continuity that Siloe had intended between the altar and the space of the ambulatory.

The longitudinal body of the cathedral – which measure 380.5 x 220.8 ft (116 x 67.3 m), with a height of 98.4 ft (30 m) – is interspersed with twenty majestic cluster pillars with Corinthian half-columns leaning against them, supporting Gothic-style vaults from an earlier period (perhaps dating from between 1575 and 1582). The classical look of the

143 top ■ **Alonso Cano's original façade adapted classical-derived elements to traditional Spanish architecture. It has since been the object of numerous imitations.**

143 bottom ■ **The aerial view shows how the space of the cathedral is structured: the volumes of the central nave, transept and the Capilla Mayor.**

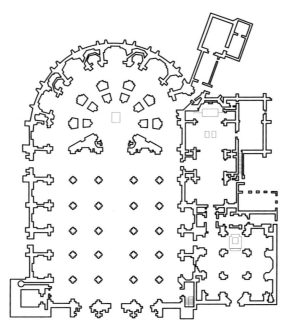

144 top ■ Annexed onto the right-hand side of the cathedral proper are the earlier building of the Capilla Real (top) and the later addition of the Sagrario (bottom).

144 bottom ■ In the central nave, the cluster pillars with Corinthian half-columns against them support the system of arcades, which in turn support the cross vaults. The Capilla Mayor is visible in the background.

145 ■ This picturesque view of the central nave and the transept emphasizes the design of the Gothic-style ribbing in the cross vaults.

Location	Style	Surface area	Type	Built
Granada (Spain)	Renaissance-Baroque	92,586 ft²	Longitudinal plan	16th-18th centuries

columns thus contrasts with Gothic elements, with a taste for the medley of styles that was typical of Spanish culture. In 1664 the great court artist Alonso Cano, a painter and architect, designed the cathedral's façade. It was completed in 1684 after his death, and is considered one of the masterpieces of the Spanish Baroque. The structure of the façade derives from a combination of the Roman triumphal arch motif (already used by Leon Battista Alberti for the façades of his churches in Mantua and Rimini) and the typical "funnel-shaped portal" that was commonly used in Spain from the Middle Ages onwards. By setting the wall back from the impost of the arches, a picturesque chiaroscuro effect is achieved, accentuating the façade's molded aspects.

Designed by the Andalusian artist Francisco de Hurtado Izquierdo, the Sagrario was built between 1704-59. Standing adjacent to the cathedral's façade, it is a square vaulted space, with a Plateresco-style dome on pendentives supported by huge cluster pillars; the pillars echo the shapes of those used by Siloe, and thus fit in with the architecture of the cathedral.

146-147 ■ This pictures shows the famous funeral monument of Ferdinand of Aragon and Isabella of Castile, inside the Capilla Real.

146 bottom ■ This photo highlights one of the elegant Gothic-style cross vaults in the Capilla Real.

147 bottom ■ The entrance from the cathedral transept into the Capilla Real is the site of precious reliefs and sculpture groups.

ST. BASIL'S
CATHEDRAL

[MOSCOW ■ RUSSIA]

On one side of Red Square, not far from the Kremlin's Spasskaya Tower, stands one of the most famous monuments in Moscow: St. Basil's Cathedral. It was originally dedicated to the Intercession, but is popularly known by the name of the saint for whom the church's tenth chapel was built. It is said that the cathedral stands on the site of a previous church built of timber, which had a cemetery where it is thought the mystic St. Basil was buried. Basil died in the odor of sanctity after having predicted the crime which would taint the Tsar, Ivan IV the Terrible when he killed his own firstborn son in a fit of rage.

In fact Ivan the Terrible had the cathedral built between 1555 and 1561, following his victory over the Tartars after a lengthy period of conflict. The Tsar wished to celebrate the invasion of the city of Kazan by erecting a spectacular building that would immortalize his memory; similarly, in Dyakovo, he commissioned the church of the Decapitation of St. John the Baptist to celebrate the birth of Ivan, his firstborn son who he would later murder. Legend has it that the Tsar used the Russian architects Barma and Postnik to build St. Basil's, and that he later had them blinded to prevent

148 ■ This detail shows the bright colors of the whimsical onion domes – called *lukovitsi* – which were added at the end of the 16th century to replace the previous ones, which were more simple in shape.

149 ■ The domes' different heights – as well as their different shapes – were designed to highlight the main tower, which rises in the center and is the fulcrum of the entire composition.

150 top ■ The interior view of the dome on the main tower shows how inside it narrows from the bottom towards the top, and the system of windows that shed light onto the chapel below.

them from ever creating a more magnificent building for anybody else. The plan of the cathedral is formed by the intersection of two squares, one of which is rotated by 45°: this creates a symmetrical structure made up of eight chapels, situated in each of the eight tips formed by the intersection, and an octagonal central space. The idea was that within one complex structure there would be nine smaller churches. Each of these was to have a tower above it and be dedicated to the saints celebrated on the days of the most important events leading to the fall of Kazan. For example, the northeastern chapel commemorates St. Gregory the Armenian, who is celebrated on 30 September 1552; that was the day in which a breach was opened in the city walls, which

proved crucial to the victory. This composition pivots around the central chapel, which commemorates the successful attack; the day fell on 1 October 1552, the feast day of the Intercession of the Virgin Mary. The only exception to this rule is the ninth chapel; the architects included it to make the design symmetrical, and it is dedicated to Christ's entry into Jerusalem. The chapels are connected by a covered roof-terrace that can be reached via two covered staircases. The elevation of the cathedral is thus influenced by the layout of the chapels. Depending on their size, the chapels are topped with octagonal towers, similar to the central one, or circular towers; all of the towers finish in brightly colored onion-shaped domes. The different heights of the towers were in

150 bottom ■ The interior of the south-eastern chapel has an original vaulted structure, with a spiral shape.

150-151 ■ The cathedral stands near the Kremlin's Spasskaja Tower. With its brightly colored skyline it stands out dramatically against the snowy mantle of the Russian winter.

LOCATION	STYLE	SURFACE AREA	TYPE	BUILT
MOSCOW (RUSSIA)	RENAISSANCE	63,507.07 FT²	CENTRAL PLAN	16TH CENTURY

fact carefully studied following a proportional system, alternating the lesser and greater heights around the highest tower, which is in the center. The latter is topped with a spire embellished with small semicircular ribbed arches known as *kokoshniki*, and towards its point has a gilded onion dome.

The lower towers are decorated with the same motif of three orders of small arches supporting the short cylindrical drum which culminates in the onion dome; meanwhile, geometrical motifs define the taller towers, where a single order of small arches supports the octagonal drum ending in a two-color onion dome. The domes were introduced in the late 16th century, replacing the less appealing ones that were there previously. In the next century, decorative panels were inserted in the *kokoshniki* and the cathedral's exterior was painted in its current colors of brick red and white, which were rediscovered during recent restoration work.

152 top ■ The photo shows detail of the frescoes that decorate some parts of the church

152 bottom ■ The decorations and furnishings are particularly lavish.

153 ■ The frescoed decoration, of which a detail is shown here, stands out for its strong colors.

ST. PAUL'S
CATHEDRAL

[LONDON ▪ UNITED KINGDOM]

A Baroque masterpiece, the Anglican cathedral of St. Paul in London was rebuilt after the Great Fire in 1666, which destroyed the previous church; it had already been built on a large scale to compete with the royal church of Westminster Abbey, dedicated to St. Peter. One of England's greatest architects, Sir Christopher Wren, was commissioned to redesign the cathedral; his vast wealth of knowledge, acquired through long periods of study and many journeys abroad, embraced both the Italian and French architecture of the time.

In 1673, Wren presented his first design to replace the ruined building; the wooden mock-up, known as the Great Model, is still on display inside the cathedral. This first design, which Wren preferred, was inspired by the basilica of St. Peter in Rome; it introduced the Greek cross floor plan, which had a large dome over the crossing. However, the design did not suit the requirements of the Anglican Church, nor was it in the tradition

154 ▪ The cathedral's façade is flanked by two tall Borromini-style towers. It has a double order of coupled Corinthian columns, and ends in a tympanum decorated with a bas-relief illustrating the Conversion of St. Paul.

155 ▪ The aerial view of the cathedral shows clearly the longitudinal layout and the importance given to the large dome, which stands above the crossing between nave and transept.

156 top and bottom left ■ Wren carefully studied the structure of the dome, and the drawing at the top shows a double-shell solution; meanwhile, the drawing below shows a cross-section of the cathedral according to the final design, with the three-shell system which forms the dome's structure.

of the English Gothic, as its nave and choir were too small. In 1675, then, Wren was obliged to resort to

156 bottom right ■ This section – of a design that was never executed – illustrates an extradosed dome with a double internal shell.

157 ■ This external view of the dome, which is covered with sheets of lead and supported by a double drum, hides the structural complexity it contains within it, and emphasizes its imposing mass. The Stone and Golden Galleries have walkways at 178 and 280 ft (54.3 and 85.4 m) above ground level.

a longitudinal floor plan with three naves, a sort of first transept placed inside the entrance, a second, short transept in the middle and a tall spire standing over the crossing, instead of the dome. Known as the Warrant Design, it was later altered, as Wren was granted the freedom to "continue this work adding any ornamental and structural variations" considered necessary. Thus the architect replaced the spire with another dome, positioned over the center of the crossing of the nave and transept, almost as a compromise with the original design. The dome is similar to that of the Dôme des Invalides in Paris. Indeed, it sits on a double drum which is colonnaded in the lower portion and set back in the upper portion. The gallery around the second drum can be walked around, as can that at the base of the lantern; they are called the Stone Gallery and Golden Gallery respectively.

The complex structure of the dome is set above eight sturdy pillars, aligned with those in the naves; they are connected by round arched arcades and covered with Corinthian pilaster strips.

The dome's construction is particularly remarkable, as it consists of three shells placed over each other: the first, hemispherical shell is pierced in the center with an oculus that provides a view of the second, conical shell; the latter was built to support the lantern as well as acting as a support for the

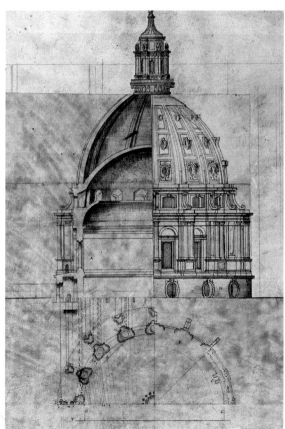

third shell, which is in wood covered with lead sheets, with a raised crown so that it is visible from afar. This complex structure, which is undetectable from the exterior, is a feature that firmly places this cathedral in the Baroque period; similarly, the main façade is flanked by two towers topped with tall spires, reminiscent of Borromini's designs. Between the towers is a deep portico and a loggia on the upper floor, both of which are supported by coupled columns; a long staircase provides access to the portico. The right hand tower is known as the Clock Tower, but it also houses the enormous Great Paul bell, cast in 1881 and weighing 17 tons. A triangular tympanum, decorated with a bas-relief depicting the conversion of St. Paul, tops the central part of the façade. Above it rises the imposing dome, which stands some 365.8 ft (111.5 m) high, with a diameter of 101.7 ft (31 m). The interior is impressively large too, measuring 479 x 124.6 ft (146 by 38 m), extending to a width of 226.3 ft (69 m) in the central transept.

People have been visiting the cathedral since it was completed in 1720. Its crypt, beneath the presbytery, houses the tombs of several illustrious figures, including Admiral Nelson, the painter William Turner and the architect of the cathedral, Sir Christopher Wren. The architect's epitaph reads: "Reader, if you seek his monument, look around," alluding to his majestic architectural achievement of St. Paul's.

159 bottom ■ The interior of the nave shows a sequence of ribbed vaults without frescoes, contrasting with the sumptuous decoration which begins at the octagon above the crossing.

160-161 ■ The dome reaches a height of 218 ft (66.5 m) above ground level, and is remarkable for its ornate monochrome frescoes, by James Thornhill.

158 ■ The ceiling of the cathedral's presbytery and choir has coffered barrel vaults and richly decorated ribbed vaults.

159 top ■ This detail shows the octagonal base of the crossing, over which rises the dome. The design of the floor emphasizes the octagonal floor plan.

Location	Style	Surface area	Type	Built
LONDON (UNITED KINGDOM)	BAROQUE	75,347.37 FT²	LONGITUDINAL PLAN	1675-1710

METROPOLITAN
CATHEDRAL

[MEXICO CITY ■ MEXICO]

Mexico City's first cathedral was built between 1524 and 1532 in the years immediately following the Spanish conquest, by order of the commander Hernán Cortés. It was situated in the heart of the holy center of what had thus far been the capital of the Aztec Empire, México-Tenochtitlán. It was deliberately built close to the Templo Mayor to assert the Catholic Church's superiority over the paganism practiced by the indigenous peoples.

Just a few years later, the first cathedral was deemed insufficient and inadequate for the ambitions of New Spain. So, from 1573, work began on the current building. Its position was moved too, albeit not very far. Due to the geological features of the land, the foundation work took a long time and the cathedral was only finished in 1793. Over the course of nearly two centuries the huge structure gradually took on the stylistic features of the different historical periods. Thus late-Baroque and Neo-Classical elements were layered over a Baroque-style plan, creating an original blend of architectural languages. The building of the Sagrario (the Sacristy) in the period 1749-68 was a later addition to the eastern side of the cathedral; it was placed next to

162 ■ The aerial view shows the architectural complex of the Metropolitan Cathedral, with the Sagrario next to it.

163 ■ The façade of the Sagrario and its extraordinarily sumptuous sculptures, are a typical example of the Mexican *churrigueresco* style.

the second chapel, and was intended to hold the holy vestments, the treasure and the archbishop's archive.

The Metropolitan Cathedral and the Sagrario attached form a single monumental façade that defines the north side of Mexico City's main Square, la Plaza de la Constitución (also known as the Zocalo) – one of the largest squares in the world. Other public buildings stand on the other sides of the square, including – on the east side – the imposing mass of the Palacio Nacional: it is home to the presidency of the Republic and its façade is some 656 ft (200 m) in length.

Unlike the curved plans typical of the Spanish and European Baroque, the cathedral in Mexico City has a rectilinear floor-plan; this is typical of most Mexican Baroque churches, and suits the grid-like shape of the urban fabric in Mexico City. The inner space consists of a large rectangular body (387 x 177 ft/118 x 54 m) divided into three naves with fourteen side-chapels, a non-projecting transept and a polygonal apse. Aligned with the main entrance are the choir, which occupies part of the central nave; the space beneath the dome, which stands at the crossing between the central nave and transept; and lastly, near the apse, the Capilla de los Reyes. The chapel is famous for its monumental 18th-century altarpiece by the Sevillian Jerónimo de Balbás: it is a large gilded wooden board overloaded with relief decorations, embellished with two paintings by Juan Rodríguez Juárez and placed to great dramatic effect behind the altar. The cathedral's monumental façade reflects the division of the inner space into naves and side-chapels. It has a tripartite central section flanked by the two massive bell towers. The dome rises up in the background. This composition of volumes reinterprets a model that was emblematic of the European Baroque and perfected in Rome by Gian Lorenzo Bernini. Here, however, it has been adapted to a flat surface, rich in architectural elements taken from different styles.

The Sagrario was designed by the Andalusian architect Lorenzo Rodríguez. It has a highly original, sumptuous façade in the Mexican *churrigueresco* style. With its jagged outline and vast stone altarpiece crowded by sculpture groups, it provides a contrast to the more rigid, static façade of the cathedral itself.

164 ■ The photograph shows the famous 18th century altar of the Capilla de los Reyes, inside the cathedral, by the Andalusian artist Jeronimo de Balbas.

165 top ■ Inside the Sagrario is the Altar of Forgiveness, with the large altarpiece behind it, embellished with paintings, sculpture groups and gilded decorations.

165 bottom ■ A worshipper deep in prayer in front of one of the large altars inside the cathedral. It is the capital's main Catholic place of worship.

Location	Style	Surface area	Type	Built
Mexico City (Mexico)	Renaissance-Baroque	75,347.37 ft²	Longitudinal plan	16th-18th centuries

VIERZEHNHEILIGEN

[LICHTENFELS ■ GERMANY]

The basilica and sanctuary of Vierzehnheiligen stands on a hill overlooking the River Main, and is dedicated to the Fourteen Holy Helpers who, together with the Christ Child, appeared to a shepherd in 1445. That episode gave rise to an initial holy building; however, by the early 18th century it was no longer large enough to accommodate the pilgrims that came to visit the sacred site. The young abbot Stephan Mösinger therefore decided to build a new church that would be adequate for the large numbers of visitors. Various building experts were called upon, including Balthasar Neumann, who was the court architect to the Prince Bishop Friedrich Karl von Schönborn, and Gottfried Heinrich Krohne, the abbot's own trusted master builder. Whereas the former delivered a design that respected the indications of the Catholic rite, the latter, a Protestant, devised a central floor plan that was deemed unsuitable by the Prince Bishop. So it was Neumann's proposal that was accepted in 1742. Neumann had already built up some previous experience in the field, as he had worked with Johann Dientzenhofer, who had designed brilliant spatial solutions for Baroque churches, and had visited Vienna, Northern Italy, Paris and Bohemia. In Vierzehnheiligen the architect brought to fruition his study of a blend of the Latin-cross floor plan with a central plan organism, which

166 ■ The plan could be described as a Latin-cross. It is made up of a series of three linked ellipses arranged lengthways; these are joined by two circles on the cross-axis to form the transept. The central oval is the fulcrum of the composition, and houses the Altar of the Fourteen Holy Helpers. The bearing structure consists of the perimeter walls as well as the pillars that mark out the elliptical spaces of the nave.

167 ■ The sober façade, which is slightly convex at the center, is flanked by twin towers. It emanates a remarkably accentuated sense of verticality and elegance.

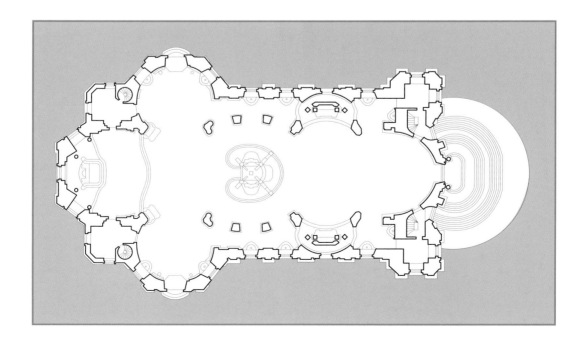

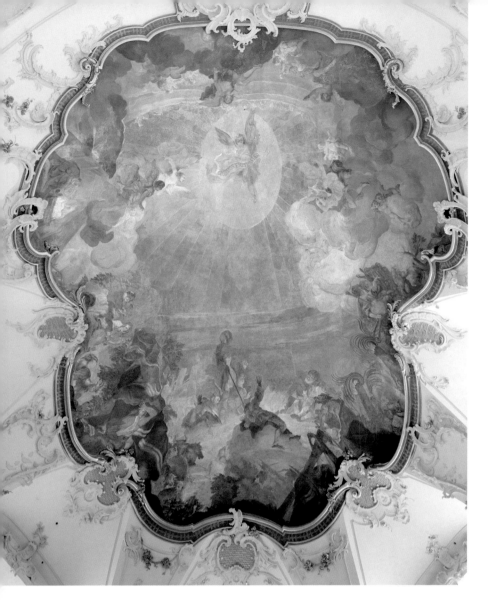

168 ■ Large windows shed light onto the brightly colored fresco by Giuseppe Appiani, painted on the vault above the High Altar. The vaults are defined by a system of double-curve longitudinal and transverse arches which are set above pilasters.

he had begun with the parish churches of Heusenstamm, Etwashausen and Gaibach. The larger scale of this building offered him new expressive possibilities, which he also explored in the contemporary designs for the Jesuits' church in Mainz (which was built and later demolished), those for Würzburg and for the monastery in Langheim (which were never built).

Vierzehnheiligen is therefore the only church that is a concrete example of this compositional logic; it is founded on the free spatial composition of the nave, using a system of pilasters and columns, separated from the traditional masonry housing. The first design for the sanctuary had a Latin-cross floor plan with a dome supported by coupled columns aligned with those in the nave, above the crossing and on the point on which the Fourteen Saints appeared. It was the intervention of Neumann's rival Krohne – who the abbot had in any case appointed as project supervisor – that led to the definitive solution. Indeed, Krohne did not follow Neumann's drawings exactly, and moved the foundations of the presbytery toward the east, thus changing the position of the altar. Neumann was forced to arrange the longitudinal layout by linking three elliptical spatial units within it, defined by pilasters and columns that stand apart from the perimeter walls. He made the central oval dominant, placing the heart-shaped altar of the Fourteen Saints within it; meanwhile the first oval became the entrance atrium and the third became the presbytery; two chapels were created between the outside walls and the pilasters. The transept, on the other hand, is structured by the outside walls and is based on a series of connected circular spaces. This unusual arrangement led to the dome being eliminated, and the oval spaces being covered with barrel vaults supported by double-curve longitudinal and transverse arches, arranged over a segmented trabeation around the perimeter. Lavish stucco moldings and precious decorations embellish the sumptuous, refined interior; this contrasts with the austere, measured sobriety of the main façade, which is flanked by two tall bell towers. With its balanced display of serenity on the exterior, and exuberant expression of divine joy in its interior, Vierzehnheiligen is the unsurpassed masterpiece of Balthasar Neumann and one of the very finest examples of the late German Baroque.

169 ■ The church's interior is sumptuously decorated with stucco friezes and moulding, culminating in the heart-shaped Altar of the Fourteen Holy Helpers, which is a dazzling expression of divine joy.

Location	Style	Surface area	Type	Built
Lichtenfels (Germany)	Baroque	20,451.43 FT²	Longitudinal plan	1743-1772

ST. ISAAC'S
CATHEDRAL

[SAN PETERSBURG ■ RUSSIA]

The Orthodox cathedral of St. Isaac (1818-1858) is a vast building topped with a gilded dome. It stands between Decembrist Square and St. Isaac Square, not far from the river Neva. It was in fact along the river bank that Tsar Peter the Great had had a previous church built in wood; he dedicated it to St. Isaac because according to the Orthodox calendar, the Tsar shared his birthday with the saint's feast day. The church collapsed in 1710 and was rebuilt in masonry by the German architect Georg Johann Mattarnovi; however, subsequent structural problems and a fire caused it to be demolished. Catherine II (1729-1796) then intervened; in memory of Peter, she entrusted the project to the Italian Antonio Rinaldi. The new building was begun on the site of the existing one, but Rinaldi's other commitments slowed work down, and his sudden death meant it was left unfinished. The Tsarina's successor, Paul I (1796-1801), chose Vincenzo Brenna to continue with the project, but fate intervened to cause another interruption: Paul I was murdered and succeeded by his first-born son, Alexander I (1801-1825), who had the building demolished as he deemed it unsuitable.

In 1809, a competition was announced to build a fourth,

170 ■ The view from the top of the cathedral shows its central plan: it is a Greek cross with arms that are almost all the same length, and has four porticoes supported by colossal columns hewn from single blocks of red granite.

171 ■ The dome of the cathedral was inspired by the celebrated domes of St. Peter's in Rome and St. Paul's in London, and further embellished with its precious gilded covering. The structure is made up of three shells placed one over the other over a double drum, the base of which is supported by red granite Corinthian columns.

172 and 173 ■ This view of the crossing highlights the ornate decorations that continue throughout the cathedral: frescoes, sculptures and paintings by various artists, most notably the painters Karl Briullov and Fedor Bruni, as well as the sculptor Ivan Vitali.

majestic cathedral on the ruins of the old one. The young French architect Auguste Ricard de Montferrand was chosen for the job. It was only in 1818, following Napoleon's campaign and after a large-scale pilework project on the site, that work began on the imposing structure, with a Greek-cross floor plan (311.6 x 344.4 ft/95 x 105 m). It is said that over 10,000 tons of timber and 300,000 tons of marble and granite went into making the building, which rises some 333 ft (101.5 m) in height from ground level to the top of its dome. The fine quality stone was shipped in from Vyborg in Finland.

The monumental ribbed dome is supported by a high colonnaded drum and topped with a lantern; it recalls that in St. Peter's in Rome, and its reinterpretation in St. Paul's Cathedral in London. It consists of three shells mounted one inside the other and measures 82 ft (25 m) in diameter; with its gilded covering it became the symbol of the city, and can be seen for miles around – even from the Gulf of Finland. Four mighty porticos lead into the arms of the Greek-cross structure; they are embellished with triangular tympanums with bronze high-reliefs by Ivan Vitali and François Lemaire. Three sides (north, south, west) are accessed via wide granite steps leading to the entrances to the church. The main entrances are on the northern and southern porticos, which are larger and have a triple row of eight pillars, flanked by two square bell towers. The eastern and western porticos, on the other hand, have just one row of eight pillars, and the eastern portico, which houses the altar, has a triple window. These colossal Corinthian pillars in Finnish red marble (52.4 ft/16 m) tall and almost 6.5 ft/2 m in diameter) ensure that the porticos are supported. The shafts of the pillars are formed from a single piece of marble resting on a bronze plinth; the capitals are also in bronze. The interior was designed to hold up to 14,000 people standing, as worshippers do not sit during ceremonies in the Orthodox rite. The floors, walls, arches and pillars are all lavishly decorated using fourteen different kinds of marble, as well as jasper, malachite, azurite, stucco, frescoes and mosaics. The vast number of icons and paintings in the Cathedral were scattered during the October 1917 Revolution. St. Isaac's was closed by the Soviets in 1931; to demonstrate the rotation of the earth, they hung a Foucault's pendulum from the top of the dome. The Cathedral was turned into a museum during the Perestroika years, before being returned to the Orthodox Church.

Location	Style	Surface area	Type	Built
St. Petersburg (Russia)	Neo-Classical	63,507.07 ft²	Greek-cross plan	1818-1858

BASILICA OF
SAN GAUDENZIO

[NOVARA ■ ITALY]

Starting in 1577, the Romanesque Basilica of San Gaudenzio in Novara was totally rebuilt to a design by Pellegrino Tibaldi. The renovated basilica had a Latin cross floor plan with a single nave and side chapels, a projecting transept and a semi-circular apse. Benedetto Alfieri built the bell tower in 1763; but it was only from 1840 onwards that the Board of Trustees tackled the problem of building the dome – already included in the 16th-century design – which had remained unresolved for over two centuries. Indeed, while waiting for the building's completion, all that had been built above the 17th-century large arches and pendentives was a modest frescoed ceiling.

The process of designing and building the dome was a lengthy and complex one. The task was given to the Piedmontese architect Alessandro Antonelli. With constant interruptions to the work and rehashes of the design, the job took him over thirty years. It was finally completed in 1878 when the lantern was built. The dome of San Gaudenzio – like the Mole Antonelliana in Turin (1862-69) – is the most remarkable achievement of Antonelli's late Neo-Classical architecture. It was to become the symbol of the city of Novara.

When drawing up the plans for the dome, Antonelli immediately had to deal with a series of technical and formal issues: the narrow proportions of the dome's circular impost; the considerable size of the main body of the basilica; the distance between the two impost levels – internal

← →

174 ■ The image shows the soaring profile of the dome of San Gaudenzio.

175 top ■ This drawing by Antonelli refers to the fifth version of the design for the dome.

175 bottom ■ The plan for San Gaudenzio was drawn up by Pellegrino Tibaldi in the 16th century.

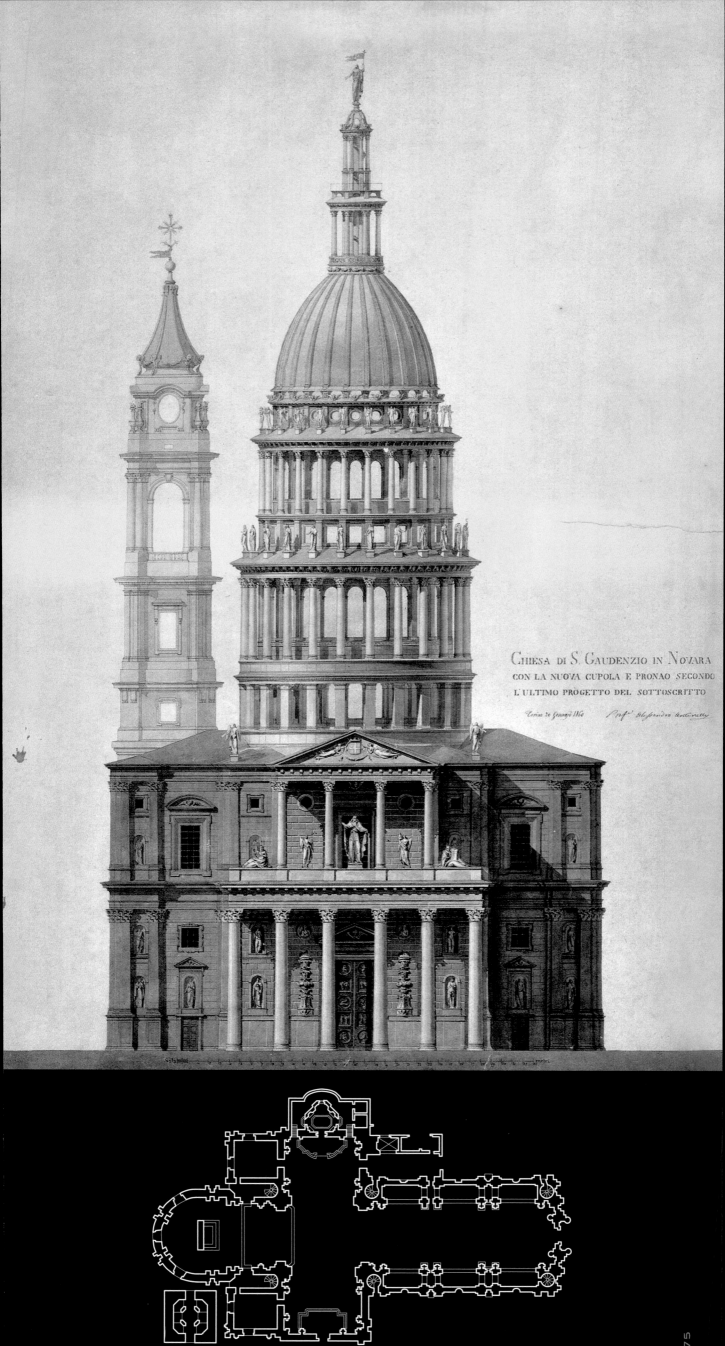

CHIESA DI S. GAUDENZIO IN NOVARA
CON LA NUOVA CUPOLA E PRONAO SECONDO
L'ULTIMO PROGETTO DEL SOTTOSCRITTO

176 ■ In this cross section of the basilica dated 1877, Leandro Caselli shows the internal structure of the various domes, built one over the other in sequence.

and external – of the dome. In order to solve these problems, he devised and perfected, through no less than eight projects (1841-61) an unprecedented construction system. He also overcame extraordinary structural difficulties, considering that the entire dome is made completely out of brickwork.

Looking at the basilica from the outside, Antonelli's architectural feat appears to be a vast cylinder topped by a dome with a lantern that reaches 400 ft (122 m) in height – markedly taller than Alfieri's bell tower. The cylindrical body is in turn made up of two peristyles of classical Corinthian columns that stand respectively on two stylobates with windows alternated with pilaster strips. The two peristyles are covered with truncated

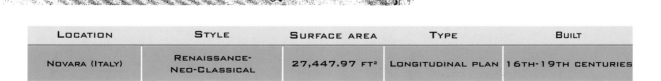

Location	Style	Surface area	Type	Built
Novara (Italy)	Renaissance-Neo-Classical	27,447.97 ft²	Longitudinal plan	16th-19th centuries

cone-shaped roofs faced in stone slabs, one set farther back than the other; they house the basements for the statues. The second peristyle is followed by an attic level with round windows, and then comes the dome proper, made up of 24 masonry segments joined by horizontal ribs. The design is then completed by a soaring lantern with a telescopic structure, which further emphasizes its verticality. With this complex scenic device, Antonelli distanced the dome from the body of the basilica, raising it toward the heavens; he thus adapted it not only to the size of the building, but also to the scale of the city and surrounding area.

This dome is not what visitors see on the interior. A cross-section of the building shows that the cylindrical body contains a series of several domes, placed one over the other: the actual coffered dome itself, placed on a colonnaded drum (contained in the first peristyle on the exterior), is followed by a second internal shell, supported by high brick ribs (contained in the second peristyle on the exterior); this is followed by a conical scaffolding of leaning piers which supports the external dome though a system of overturned arches.

In its external appearance, Antonelli's dome picks up on various formal solutions used in some of the most famous domes of the time – those of St. Paul's in London, Sainte-Geneviève's in Paris. However, its complex internal arrangement evokes, two centuries later, the structural tradition of the famous baroque domes of Guarino Guarini

WESTMINSTER
CATHEDRAL

[LONDON ■ UNITED KINGDOM]

This Cathedral in London is the largest Catholic church in the United Kingdom, and is also the seat of the Archbishop of Westminster. Next to the main altar there is even a copy of the Pope's throne (the original is at St. John Lateran in Rome, the church in which the Pope serves as bishop of Rome). The cathedral stands in the heart of the city, near Victoria Station, on land which previously belonged to Westminster Abbey but was sold in the 17th century to build a prison; the Catholic church bought the land in 1884. In 1850 Pope Pius IX had reintroduced the the Catholic hierarchy; he set up the Diocese of Westminster and appointed the first Archbishop. Herbert Vaughan, the third Archbishop, therefore wished to build a majestic new building that would be the outward expression of the Catholic faith: and so he assigned the task to John Francis Bentley, an architect who was well known in Victorian times for his designs of religious buildings.

This was the architect's first ever project in the Neo-Byzantine style, symbolizing the resurgence of Catholicism in London. Bentley therefore made his own Grand Tour in the Mediterranean region. As his main sources he chose Hagia Sophia in Istanbul, the basilica of San Vitale in Ravenna and St. Mark's in Venice. Indeed, the interior, which was completed at a later date, is full

178 ■ This aerial view of the cathedral gives an idea of its imposing longitudinal plan, with its unusual sequence of slightly jutting domes, which are in keeping with the Byzantine inspiration behind the design.

179 ■ This view of the façade and side of the cathedral accentuates the contrast between the horizontality of the main body, and the verticality of the bell tower.

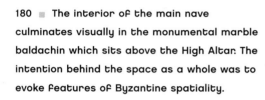 180 ■ The interior of the main nave culminates visually in the monumental marble baldachin which sits above the High Altar. The intention behind the space as a whole was to evoke features of Byzantine spatiality.

181 ■ This view of the interior of the Lady Chapel, whose vaulted ceiling is visible at the bottom, highlights the rich decorations inspired by the interiors of Justinian's churches. The designer used the same mosaic technique on a gold background.

of precious materials and fine Byzantine-style mosaics: the architect used around one hundred different types of marble, and for the eight pillars in the nave he chose the same green marble that was used in St. Sophia's.

The cathedral was built quickly. Only eight years passed between the day the foundation stone was laid in 1895 and the building's completion. It has a triple-apsed basilical floor plan with deep chapels and ambulatory formed from the thickness of the outside walls; a sort of narthex leads to the spacious nave, which extends for no less than 360.8 ft (110 m); it can hold a seated congregation of up 1200 people, in addition to several hundred standing in the galleries above the aisles. Along the nave is a series of lighting pendants; there were designed by Bentley, Son & Marshall, modeled on the metal circles that held the candles in Hagia Sophia. The Stations of the Cross, meanwhile, are by Eric Gill and were fitted during the First World War. The fifty thousand Irish soldiers who lost their lives in that war are commemorated in one of the side-chapels, which is dedicated to St. Patrick.

At the end of the nave stands the High Altar. It is decorated by a crucifix and six candelabra which were also designed by the architect and his team; a baldacchino on marble pillars rises above the altar, and is surmounted by another Crucifix, which was made in Bruges. The latter stands out against the background of a dome resting on pendentives, at the base of which runs a series of openings which let in natural light; the overall effect is one of radiance, once again inspired by the example of Hagia Sophia. The exterior is faced with horizontal bands of open brickwork and white Portland stone; it is said that some twelve and a half million bricks were used to make it. The main façade is richly decorated, embellished by a widely splayed door and terminates in two short towers with lanterns; on the side are two smaller robust towers topped with domes, and a single bell tower – 283.7 ft/86.5 m high – which is a true landmark for this area of London.

Location	Style	Surface area	Type	Built
London (United Kingdom)	Neo-Byzantine	53,819.55 ft²	Longitudinal plan	1895-1903

the TWENTIETH CENTURY

At the dawn of the twentieth century, the famous Catalan architect Antoni Gaudí (1852-1926) was still busy building his last work, the temple of the Sagrada Familia in Barcelona.

Although it took inspiration from the Gothic, this building achieved totally original results in terms of construction and expressivity. Gaudí managed to counterbalance the weight of the vaults by sloping the pillars and using parabolic arches. He thus avoided the need for supports and buttresses, typical elements of Gothic cathedrals which he considered structural "defects".

The use of innovative construction techniques which also took on strong expressive connotations was a recurring feature of 20th-century religious architecture. The French architect Auguste Perret (1874-1954), in the church of Notre-Dame de la Consolation in Raincy (1922-23), also achieved an airy structure in reinforced concrete. In this case, the idea was to experiment with the technical potential of a new construction material. This then allowed Perret to close the shell with non-bearing walls made from prefabricated concrete modules and stained glass, again evoking a Gothic-style atmosphere.

However, in the first half of the 20th-century religious architecture was not particularly fashionable. The architects of the so-called International Style preferred projects such as homes and public buildings. A turning point came after the Second World War, when Le Corbusier (1887-1965) built the legendary chapel at Ronchamp (1950-54). In it, he removed any traditional references of type, form or style. The unbroken inclined concave and convex walls support a complexly curved roof. The result is, on the exterior, a sculpted construction with no identifiable main façade and, on the interior, a hollowed-out cave-like space, atmospherically lit by a constellation of splayed openings which erratically pierce the southern wall.

Gothic architecture had already experimented with the use of light as an element that could evoke the presence of God. In contemporary religious architecture, however, this solution took on a newly symbolic significance, going so far as to

The Twentieth Century

completely influence the inner spaces. A perfect example is Tokyo's Roman Catholic Cathedral of St. Mary, designed by Kenzo Tange (1913-2005), with its cross-shaped skylight. Or the metropolitan cathedral of Brasília by Oscar Niemeyer; here, large sloping glazed surfaces are inserted between the structure's reinforced concrete uprights, arching up towards the sky.

Let us turn to the architecture of recent years. There are two buildings which boast the greatest innovations in terms of the pioneering construction techniques which were used to create architectural spaces with a strong expressive and communicative force: these are Richard Meier's church of Dio Padre Misericordioso, built in Rome for the Jubilee; and the Sanctuary of San Pio da Pietrelcina, built in San Giovanni Rotondo by Renzo Piano. In both cases, the architects devised specific, ground-breaking technical solutions, albeit using different materials: concrete and stone. In Meier's church, the sacred space is enclosed by three vast sails, alluding to the Trinity, and by large glazed surfaces. A self-bearing structure was designed for the sails; this consists of a metal frame onto which 256 pre-fabricated double curved white concrete panels were mounted. In the Sanctuary of Padre Pio, Renzo Piano created the large parabolic arches which describe the space of the building out of a traditional material, namely stone. However, he employed it using a cutting-edge technique, so as to exploit its full potential in terms of technical performance.

BASILICA OF THE
ANNUNCIATION

[NAZARETH ■ ISRAEL]

184-185 ■ This view shows the architectural complex of
the Cathedral of the Annunciation, with the two large
churchyards at different levels and also the
Franciscan monastery next to the basilica.

In 1959 the Franciscan Order commissioned the Italian architect Giovanni Muzio to build a large basilica in one of the most ancient holy sites in Christendom: the grotto in which the Archangel Gabriel announced the conception of Jesus to Mary of Nazareth. Various structures have succeeded each other on this site over the course of the centuries a 3rd-4th century sanctuary, two medieval basilicas built one on top of the other; and a small temple built in the 18th century.

The archaeological excavations carried out between 1955-58 provided the crucial grounds for a project for a new basilica, which was to preserve and display the various archaeological finds, fit in with the existing friary and house large crowds of pilgrims.

Muzio tackled the complex project with great flair. He arranged the entire composition around the grotto of the Annunciation: two large spaces, one over the other, are connected by a large octagonal oculus. At the level of the lower church, the oculus is placed over the holy grotto, while in the upper church it is surmounted by a monumental dome, also octagonal in shape, which rises to a height of 131.2 ft (40 m) above

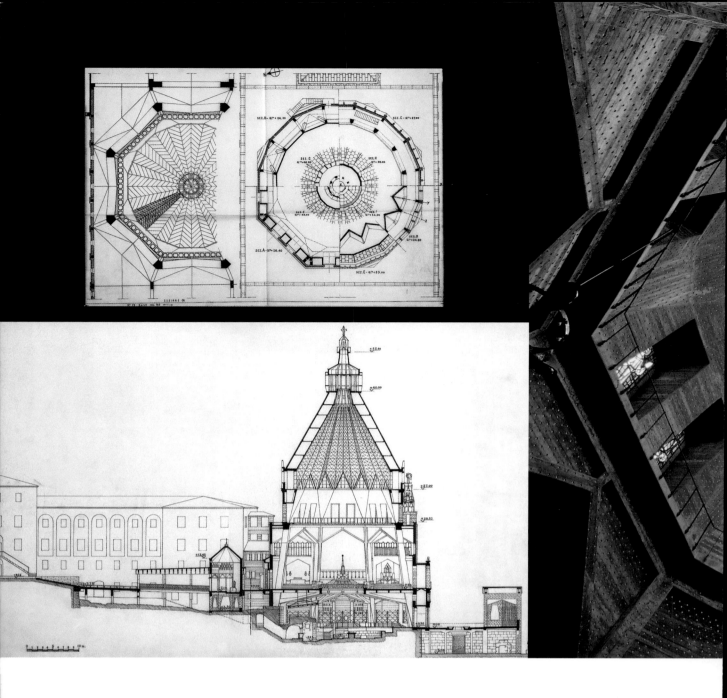

ground level. The constant reference to the octagon recalls the figure of the Virgin Mary in the Christian tradition: the 8th September is her presumed date of birth, and is also the day in which the sun enters the constellation of Virgo. This daring structure was built using a double framework of sturdy pilasters and corbels in reinforced concrete to support the floor of the upper church, and the double-shell pyramid structure of the dome. The large oculus cuts through the floor of the upper church, providing a view of the holy grotto, which is situated at the level of the lower church.

Hence both churches have a rectangular plan with a single chamber, containing a large centralized structure that focuses the attention of worshippers, pushing toward the holy grotto and the altar. The lower church follows the layout of the walls of the medieval basilica, which Muzio reused on the northern side up to a height of 9.8-13.1 ft (3-4 m.

The idea of building two churches one on top of the other recalls the arrangement of the basilica of St. Francis in Assisi. However, it also presents the opportunity to create a more intimate atmosphere around the holy grotto – in the lower church, which is conducive to individual prayer – while offering worshippers a large space – the upper church – where they can congregate during liturgical celebrations. In the lower church, the floor drops to the different levels of the archaeological remains and the pilasters slope inwards, bringing to mind a natural, primordial space such as a cave; this creates a very evocative, striking setting which recalls the very origins of Christianity.

Location	Architect	Surface area	Type	Built
Nazareth (Israel)	Giovanni Muzio	12,378.50 FT²	Longitudinal plan	1959-1969

Building two churches also allowed Muzio to carefully integrate the basilica into its surrounding landscape, and perfectly organize the system of open spaces and pathways. Indeed, on three sides the basilica is surrounded by two large squares; situated at different levels, they are situated in front of the main entrances of the two churches. The upper church is accessed on the north side via an elevated that connects it to the existing monastery. This square contains an octagonal baptistery, and protects the remains of the ancient village of Nazareth beneath it. The lower church is reached from the south and west sides (in front of the main façade) from a wide plaza. Running around it is a portico of 344.4 ft (105 m) in length which, to the south, has a loggia overlooking the valley below.

186 top ■ This drawing shows horizontal sections at different heights of the dome in the upper church.

186 bottom ■ The cross section shows how the two churches, at different levels, are placed one above the other.

186-187 ■ The large octagonal dome rises 131.2 ft (40 m) above the floor level of the upper church.

187 bottom left ■ In the background of this interior view of the lower church is the Holy Grotto of the Annunciation.

187 bottom right ■ This photograph shows the interior of the upper church.

METROPOLITAN
CATHEDRAL

[BRASILIA ■ BRAZIL]

Brasilia is a recently founded city. The city was built starting in 1960, with the aim of giving Brazil a new capital that would be free of any references to the country's past as a Portuguese colony. It was designed according to the most forward-looking principles of modern town planning. The city's plan was designed by Lucio Costa. Taking inspiration from Le Corbusier's urban projects – from the Villa Contemporaine to his projects for Montevideo, São Paulo and Rio – Costa organized the urban fabric along two axes which cross at right-angles: the large residential blocks are arranged along the longitudinal axis, which has a curved shape that adapts to the shape of the artificial lake. Meanwhile, the transverse axis is 3.1 miles (5 km) long and over 328 ft (100 m) wide; on this axis the public buildings are located.

Oscar Niemeyer, Brazil's most famous architect, was commissioned to design the public buildings including the cathedral, which is the city's masterpiece. He set himself the target of *"creating a cathedral which had no need for a cross or statues of saints to symbolize the House of God, in the manner of a monumental sculpture which translates a religious idea, a moment for prayer. A single block, pure and simple. A work of art."* (Niemeyer, 1975).

The conical shape of the building was achieved with a skeleton of 16 uprights in reinforced concrete, anchored at their base to a ring of 229.6 ft (70 m) in length. The uprights arch upwards and are secured at the top by a thin concrete disc, which they rise above, thrusting up toward the heavens. Between one upright and another are large glazed surfaces which are also sloped. The architecture is therefore totally integrated with the structural system – all the more so considering that originally the concrete was left exposed. It thus achieves the perfect *"synthesis of engineering and architecture, form and structure, technique and imagination"* that is the Brazilian master's stylistic

188-189 ■ **This external view of Metropolitan Cathedral highlights its pure lines and daring structure.**

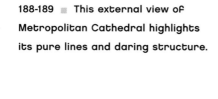

trademark. The purity of the conical shape formed by this framework could evoke the image of a crown of thorns, thus bringing to mind the passion of Christ. Or, more prosaically, the shape of a Native American teepee or even a vast tropical flower that is opening its petals. If we refer to traditional Christian architecture, the circular plan combined with vertical elements could perhaps be read as a sort of reworking or plastic deformation of the ancient temples, which had a circular floor plan and continuous colonnades. Meanwhile, the building's marked vertical tension immediately evokes the spirit of the great Gothic cathedrals.

In order to maintain the purity of this shape, the additional structures of the Baptistery and Sacristy are kept separate from the main chamber of the cathedral, and are linked to it via a pathway below street level. The entrance to the cathedral is also set into an underground passage which is approached through a sort of entrance avenue defined by the huge statues of the apostles, sculpted by Alfredo Ceschiatti. The Brazilian master architect deliberately created a contrast between the dark space of the entrance in black granite, and the explosion of light and color which greets worshippers in the main space, which is fully glazed. *"First of all, the exterior: the airy structure springing from the ground, like a cry of faith and*

hope; then, the gallery situated in the obscurity, to prepare the faithful for the religious spectacle; lastly, the contrast of light and the exterior effects, as the worshippers are distanced from the world and projected between the cathedral and infinite space" (Niemeyer, 1975). Indeed, the cathedral's interior has an unreal, almost fairytale atmosphere. This is also emphasized by the softly curved lines of the uprights that converge toward the center of the dome; while figures of angels are suspended from the top, hovering above the heads of the congregation.

190-191 ■ The inner space is enclosed within a circular hyperboloid shape. It is lit by means of large windows designed by Marianne Peretti, which replaced the originals by the same artist.

191 ■ The bell tower stands separate from the main building and echoes its architectural lines.

LOCATION	ARCHITECT	SURFACE AREA	TYPE	BUILT
BRASILIA (BRAZIL)	OSCAR NIEMEYER	41440.89 FT²	CENTRAL PLAN	1959-1970

192 ■ This aerial view shows the cross-shaped plan of St. Mary's Cathedral, defined by sloping diagonal walls and the large skylight.

192-193 ■ This exterior view of the cathedral highlights the radiant effect produced by the stainless steel facing.

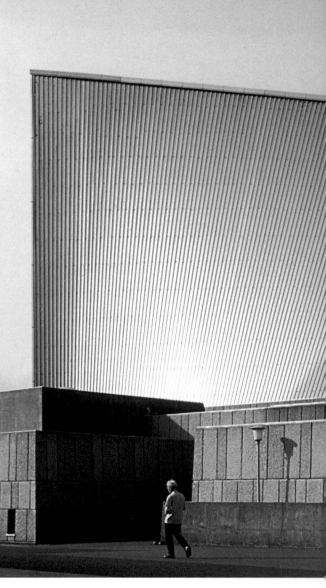

ST. MARY'S
CATHEDRAL

[TOKYO ■ JAPAN]

Tokyo's present Roman Catholic cathedral, situated in the Bunkyo-ku district, was designed by the architect Kenzo Tange. It occupies the same site on which the church of the Immaculate Virgin previously stood. The earlier church was built in 1889 and was destroyed by fire in 1945 during the Second World War.

Tange's project won a competition that was announced in 1961. This building is one of the most emblematic examples of the Japanese master architect's work. It was completed in 1964. In order to tackle this project, Tange visited some of Europe's most important Gothic cathedrals. He drew certain elements of inspiration from them, bringing them up to date in an overtly mod-

ern language. He also made use of the potential offered by new materials: *"After experiencing their heaven-aspiring grandeur and ineffably mystical spaces (...) I began to imagine new spaces, and wanted to create them by means of modern technology"* (Kenzo Tange).

The architecture of Tokyo's cathedral also expresses the overcoming of the typically functionalist style which had dominated architectural culture in the Twenties and Thirties. Le Corbusier had already launched this trend in the early Fifties with his construction, also on the theme of religion, of the chapel of Ronchamp in France. The same plastic tension which is expressed at Ronchamp by the use of geometries based on combinations of concave and convex forms, is also seen in the perimeter walls of Tokyo Cathedral, which are in the shape of eight hyperbolic paraboloids.

The plan of the cathedral is cruciform, defined by sloping diagonal walls. Geometrically shaped as hyperbolic paraboloids, the walls sweep upwards, defining the cross of light formed by the large skylight which lights the interior from above. Other openings on the four corners of the church, corresponding with the arms of the cross, cut vertically through the volume of the building, which is otherwise completely unbroken. As the form of the cathedral

makes no references to traditional ecclesiastical architecture, its recognition depends purely on the clear symbolism of the cross. Thus in this sense, the architecture takes on a strong communicative significance.

The daring structure is made from concrete. On the exterior it is clad with panels of stainless steel which react to the light, creating an evocative effect of radiance in keeping with the religious character of the building.

The architect's rejection of orthogonal forms is also immediately apparent in the interior: the high, sloping walls of the nave and the lower walls of the side areas welcome and protect worshippers as though they were in the belly of a cave; the light penetrates the interior from the large skylight in the ceiling, forming a cross shape which hovers

LOCATION	ARCHITECT	SURFACE AREA	TYPE	BUILT
TOKYO (JAPAN)	KENZO TANGE	39,288.27 FT²	LONGITUDINAL PLAN	1961-1964

over the heads of the congregation and bounces off the rough surfaces of the walls, which are finished in exposed concrete. A concrete cross also stands at the meeting point between the arms of the skylight, while another cross is placed behind the altar and is lit by one of the four vertical openings.

The cathedral can hold a seated congregation of 1500 people. It is completed by a series of secondary buildings connected to it by means of a system of pathways and platforms. The bell tower is particularly interesting; it stands apart from the main body of the cathedral and rises some 196.8 ft (60 m) up to the heavens, signaling the cathedral's presence to the city.

194-195 ■ The interior of the cathedral, with the altar. The inside walls were left as exposed concrete.

195 top ■ This photograph of the entrance shows how the walls gradually draw together towards the top.

195 bottom ■ With its characteristic cross shape, the large skylight in the roof not only lights the inner space but also takes on a clear symbolic significance.

LA GRAN MADRE DI DIO

[TARANTO ▪ ITALY]

The size and population of Taranto grew dramatically after the new Italsider steel plant was set up there in the early 1960s. As a result, Archbishop Monsignor Guglielmo Motulese decided to have a second cathedral built in a new area of the city, in addition to the ancient cathedral situated in the heart of the old town.

The project was assigned to the Milanese architect Gio Ponti. After a long design process that began in 1964, the cathedral was completed in 1971.

The architectural complex stands in the Rione Italia quarter and occupies an area of 80,730 sq. ft/7500 sq. m. The cathedral of La Gran Madre di Dio stands alone on a podium before a vast square, with a large pool of water in which the design of its façade is reflected to great dramatic effect. To the back of the cathedral, surrounded by a large garden, are the annexed buildings including the bishop's residence and other parish facilities.

196 ▪ The Façade of the Co-Cathedral of Taranto, which is mirrored in the pool of water that lies before it.

197 ▪ Above the entrance Façade is a large sail, 137.7 Ft (42 m) high and 4305.5 sq. Ft (400 sq. m) in extent, pierced by narrow rectangular and hexagonal holes which let the light shine through.

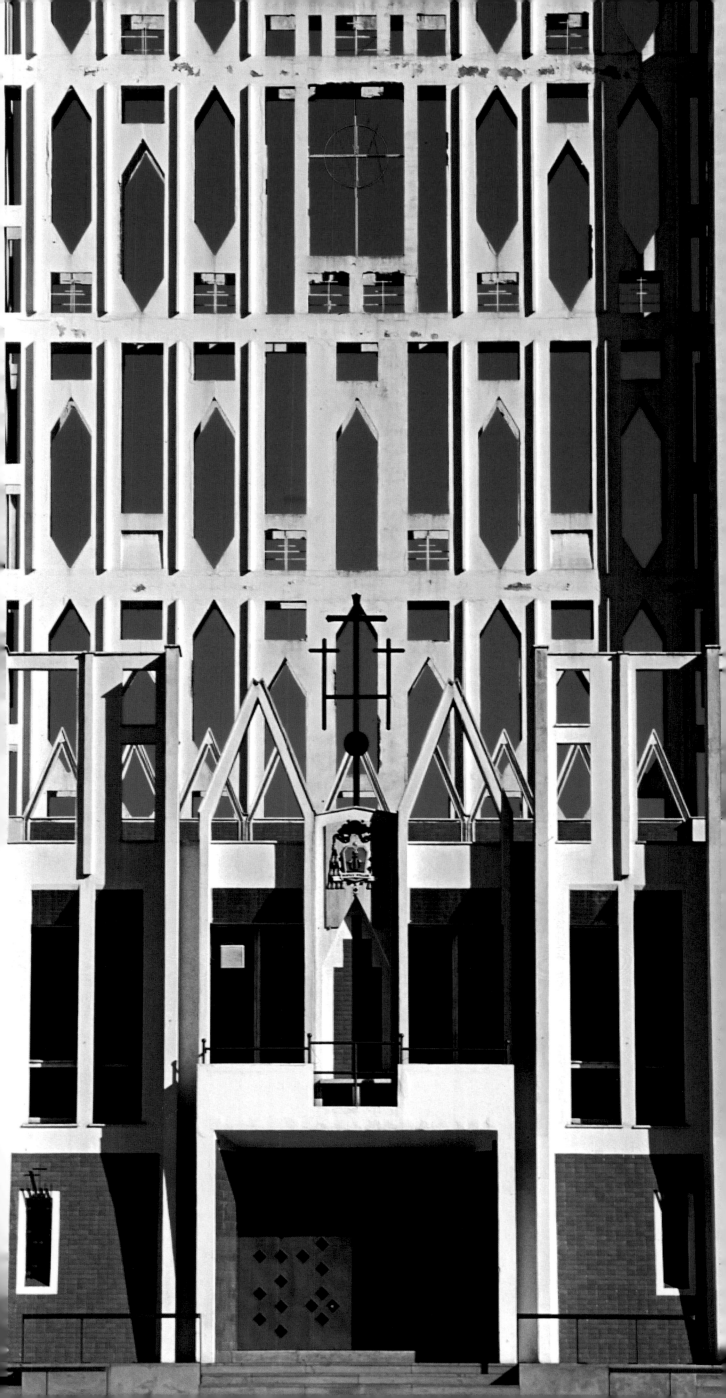

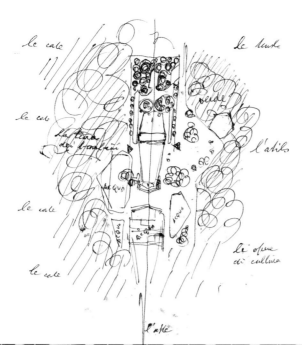

The numerous project notes show how the cathedral's architecture is the result of a tension between a horizontal structure, containing the nave, and the large vertical face which, like a sail unfurled in the wind, towers over it and is the distinguishing feature of the cathedral itself. Ponti was inspired to create this contrast by observing Romanesque, Gothic and Renaissance churches. All of these are dominated by striking vertical elements (towers, spires and extradosed domes), so that at first the sail was called a "tower" or even a "rectangular dome." Initially the sail was designed as a continuous rectangular body; but as the project evolved, it became a slim, elegant perforated screen. It acts as an airy counter-façade that contrasts with the more earthly façade of the entrance. "*I thought: two façades. One, the lower one, a staircase climbing up it to the doors of the church. The other, larger one, can only be reached by the gaze and the wind: a façade "in the air" for a cathedral flooded with air, a façade made up of twin façades, with eighty windows opening onto the "immensity" which is the "dimension" of the mystery of the eternal presence of God.*" (Gio Ponti, 1971).

Taranto Cathedral came after Ponti's experiments in Milan with the chapels of San Francesco and San Carlo. It belongs to a phase of his research in which the architectural element of the isolated, perforated wall, combined with Ponti's preference for certain recurring shapes such as the hexagon and diamond, became a screen that could transform the inner space of the church into a large box of light. Compared to the examples mentioned above, with the

façade for Taranto Cathedral Ponti accentuates the autonomous quality of the wall as though it were a vast altarpiece extended out into its environment.

Inside, the cathedral has a rectangular main chamber – 246 x 75 .5 ft (75 x 23 m); it is defined by a framework of beams and pillars in reinforced concrete. At the height of the presbytery the sail-like element rises up suddenly, flooding the altar with a celestial light. The original project intended for the cathedral's architecture to be poetically immersed in lush vegetation, which could even climb all over the large sail: *"The Cathedral's architecture will be complete – because it was designed with this in mind – when it will be under siege by the foliage of climbing plants, wildly attacked and protected by olive trees, eucalyptus, oleanders and shrubs from the land around Taranto: and it will become forest, it will bloom in springtime, it will shed leaves in the winter."* (Gio Ponti, 1971).

198 top ■ This drawing by Gio Ponti is a study for the layout of the Co-Cathedral's architectural complex. Note the pools of water and the greenery.

198 bottom ■ This photograph gives an idea of the inner space in the large rectangular hall. In the foreground, the presbytery area with light coming through the large sail.

198-199 ■ Gio Ponti has drawn over this photograph of the southern side to show vegetation "attacking" the cathedral, as planned in his original design.

Location	Architect	Surface area	Type	Built
Taranto (Italy)	Gio Ponti	18,567.75 ft²	Longitudinal plan	1964-1971

CRYSTAL

CATHEDRAL

[GARDEN GROVE ■ USA]

The cathedral owes its name to the prolific use of steel and glass that makes up the structure and facing of the building, which stands glittering under the Californian sun: Philip Johnson, the world-renowned architect who designed it, says that he was inspired by expressionist architecture, reinterpreted in a Hi-Tech style. The Crystal Cathedral was built between 1977 and 1980 for the Garden Grove religious community in California. The community's leader was the enterprising Robert Schuller, who aspired to create "a church like no other, for its congregation which is different from the others." Indeed, with its Sunday sermon broadcast over no fewer than 177 TV channels, the community had a huge number of followers. Philip Johnson, who had previously designed the Glass House in New Canaan and the AT&T building in New York, was the highly imaginative architect whom Schuller chose to interpret the particular requirements of his congregation and to express a religious feeling updated by show business and commercial awareness.

200 ■ The exterior view of the building draws attention to its smooth reflective glass surfaces: these gave it the name of "Crystal Cathedral." They enclose a space which does not blend into its surroundings, but are also an unmistakeable landmark for the religious community of Garden Grove.

201 ■ The cathedral's bell tower soars airily skywards in its steel structure, tapering up to a height of about 239.5 ft (73 m). At the top is a carillon which rings out the peals of fifty-two bronze bells.

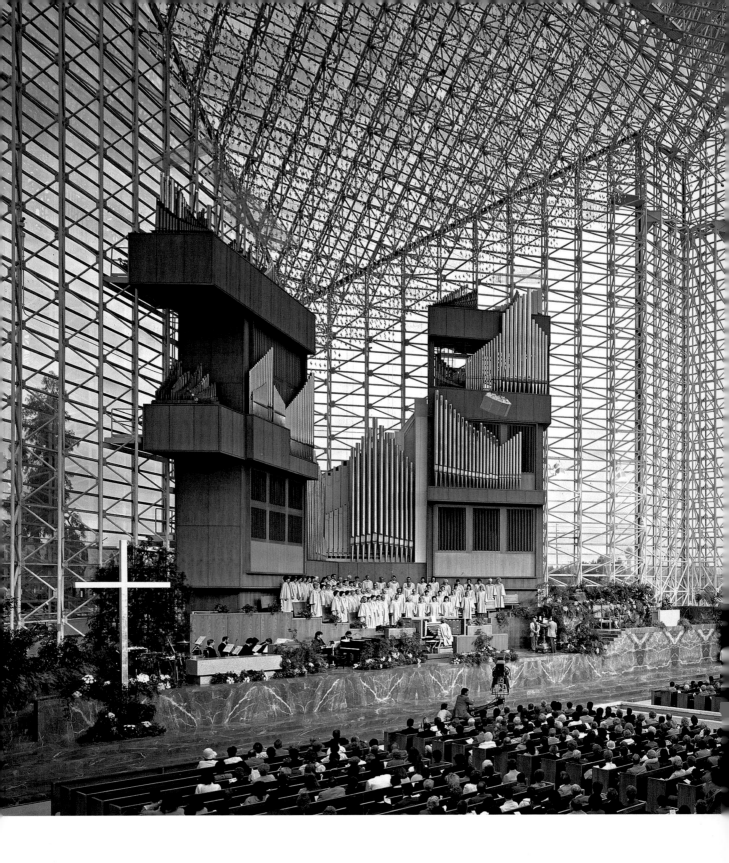

Johnson's design proved to be so effective that it replaced the previous church that Richard Neutra had designed and which had been built in 1962. The architect had the task of imagining a structure that would be able to hold 3000 worshippers, to amaze and attract the viewing public and be used to put on religious-themed shows at Christmas and Easter. In agreement with Schuller, Johnson rejected the classic longitudinal layout, which creates a distance between the faithful and the preacher; instead he devised a diamond-shaped layout, distributing the seats along the shorter axis and reducing the space lengthways by using three balconies. These are situated in three of the diamond's tips, where the faithful enter the church; the fourth tip, however, is occupied by the pulpit and a large stage for the choir, which can be used for shows broadcast on television. A vast, asymmetrical-shaped organ rises up behind the stage, standing out against the lacy network of beams that forms the building's structure. Water trickles out from a long, rectangular tank placed in front of the pulpit, as though from a fountain; but the stream of water is interrupted as soon as the minister begins to preach. Two 88.5-ft (27-m) high revolving doors – known as the Cape Canaveral Doors - are either side of the stage; these allow people to participate in the cer-

LOCATION	ARCHITECT	SURFACE AREA	TYPE	BUILT
GARDEN GROVE - CALIFORNIA (USA)	PHILIP JOHNSON ALAN RITCHIE	14,531.28 FT²	CENTRAL PLAN	1977-1982

202-203 ■ In this view, it is clear how the space was designed around the idea of the religious ceremony as a show. Note the stage, dominated by the vast organ, and one of the three balconies which overlooks the audience of worshippers, surrounded by the intricate metal truss frame of the structure.

emony from the car park, following it visually like in a drive-in, and listening on the radio. Now, more parking spaces having been added, giant screens have been installed to ensure that everyone can watch the religious show. The walls and roof, meanwhile, are made up of a tight network of metal trusses which support the glass surfaces of the exterior facing. These glass panels reflect the sunlight, helping to moderate the temperature in the church, which has no air-conditioning. An unusual system of windows that can be opened mechanically allows the church to be ventilated, while allowing the "crystalline" continuity of the outside surface to be maintained when the windows are closed. Lastly, Schuller commissioned Johnson to design the steeple, which is a steel tower standing 239.4 ft (73 m) tall; at the base is a marble chapel, while at the top, in addition to a carillon with 52 bronze bells, there is a lit signal for aircraft. This tower represents the completion of the building, which is a sort of virtual theater set in a religious context.

CATHEDRAL OF THE
RESURRECTION

[ÉVRY ■ FRANCE]

This is how the Ticino-born architect Mario Botta presented his project for the new cathedral at Évry, dedicated to St. Corbinien, in December 1988: *"Building a cathedral (...) is the desire to create a place and a space for the spirit, closely integrated with the urban fabric, which can help us to deal with daily life (...) For the architect, this means working and building in the hope of getting to grips with the need for vastness that each of us has."*

Botta thus refers to an integration between the space of the cathedral seen as the place where humans express their desire for spirituality, and the urban fabric of the city, where humans face the materiality of daily life. At Évry this integration is expressed through an architectural complex which consists of the cylindrical volume of the church and a lower building used for apartments and offices. This lower building encloses the church, forming a sort of semi-closed civic cloister. The whole complex is part of the civic center of the city of Évry (near the Town Hall, the University and

204 ■ The photograph shows a detail of Évry Cathedral's new cylindrical building, near the area behind the altar. Note the brickwork facing.

205 ■ The cathedral's cylindrical body is 126 ft (38.4 m), with a height varying between 55.7 and 111.5 ft (17 and 34 m).

the Chamber of Commerce), one of the so-called *villes nouvelles* that was built in the 1970s in the southern suburbs of Paris. With its monumental cylindrical shape, the cathedral has thus become the focal point of the new civic and religious center.

As Botta chose a centralized plan for his cathedral, he used an elementary form – the cylinder – which recurs in his civic and religious architecture; not only that, he also created a symbolic connection with the tradition of Renaissance and Early Christian centralized buildings. He conceived the cathedral as a temple, meant in the etymological sense as a "house of God"; he then extended this concept by interpreting is as the "house of people."

The cathedral's circular plan is arranged using a double shell built of reinforced concrete. Thus, the

ring around the main chamber is able to house the flight of steps connecting the two entrances placed at different heights; the staircase leading to the tribune galleries and to the roof; and other spaces including a contemporary art center. From the exterior, the building appears to be a truncated cylinder cut on the diagonal (it has a diameter of 125.8 ft (38.4 m and its height varies between 55.7 and 111.5 ft (17 and 34 m), faced in red brick. Its sloping roof is edged by a crown of 24 silvery lime trees (16.4-19.6 ft/5-6 m) tall; rising in the direction of a cross placed at the top of the roof, the trees metaphorically recall the concept of the resurrection. Each spring, they are "reborn" after having seemingly "died" during the winter months. The presence of nature as an integral part of the cathedral's architecture also acts as a reminder, through the changing seasons, of the inescapable passage of time.

The interior features curved walls dressed in red brick, and a large skylight, through which the circular chamber (internal diameter 96.1 ft/29.3 m)

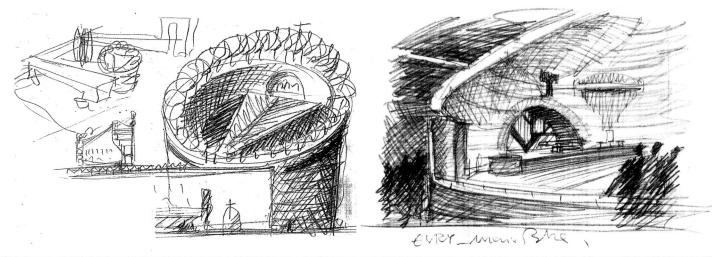

is flooded with light. The intensity of the light is controlled by aluminum slatted blinds attached to the windows. The metal structure of the ceiling consists of tubular elements that form a triangular three-dimensional shape; it is sloped at an angle of 31° to the horizontal, and rests on three reinforced concrete supports that are anchored to the walls of the cylinder.

The capacity of 800 people seated rises to 1500 if the galleries that overlook the central chamber, like boxes in a theater, are included.

The direction of the central space is indicated by the altar, behind which is a large semi-circular low window. A sort of ridged brick curtain falls from above, helping to optimize the acoustics of the space.

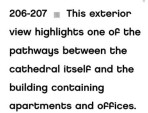

206-207 ■ This exterior view highlights one of the pathways between the cathedral itself and the building containing apartments and offices.

207 top ■ In these drawings, Mario Botta studies the arrangement of the exterior shape of the cathedral and the definition of the inner space

Location	Architect	Surface area	Type	Built
Évry (France)	Mario Botta	12,449.32 ft²	circular plan	1988-1995

SANCTUARY OF

SAN PIO
DA PIETRELCINA

[SAN GIOVANNI ROTONDO ■ ITALY]

For decades now, thousands of pilgrims have been traveling to San Giovanni Rotondo from all over Italy and the world to pay homage to Padre Pio (1887-1968). The charismatic Capuchin friar, his body marked by the mystery of the stigmata, was declared a saint in 2002. In 1991, the architect Renzo Piano was commissioned to build a new church. It would have to be capable of providing adequate prayer, meditation and reception space for the multitude of pilgrims.

The underlying idea of the design, clearly expressed from the very first sketches, was to create a large liturgical hall with a "fan-shaped" plan. A vast triangular parvis would connect it with the existing buildings – the ancient chapel, the church built in the 1950s and the Casa Sollievo della Sofferenza hospital; thus a new urban fabric would skillfully be created. The system of pedestrian links is extremely effective and visually striking. From a monumental stone cross 131.2 ft (40 m) high with arms 32.8 ft (10 m) wide, a long processional walk-

208-209 ■ The photographs shows a three-dimensional studio model of the roof system.

209 top ■ The photograph shows the actual roof system.

209 bottom ■ In this sketch, Renzo Piano defines the main elements of his design: the processional pathway, the wall, the large fan-shaped chamber.

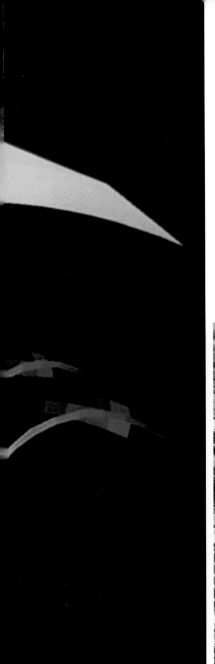

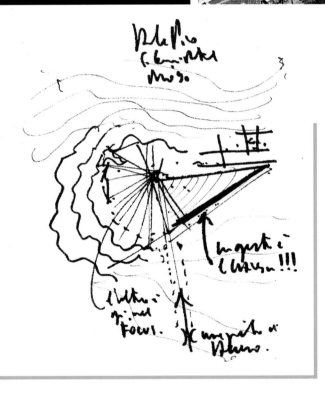

way, its first section covered with a colonnade in turn 328 ft (100 m) long, leads via a system of ramps and stairways to the vast parvis measuring 107,640 sq. ft/0,000 sq. m. It then reaches the main entrance to the church, on the opposite side. This forecourt is on a slight downward slope, as though to guide the worshippers toward the church, and acts as an open-air church in the true sense of the word. Beneath the huge upper church and parvis are two subterranean levels cut out of the mountainside. They house the lower church and other areas for receiving pilgrims.

The dominant motif of the design is the system of parabolic arches. They are arranged in a radial sequence with a steadily decreasing span of 10 degrees, around a sturdy central pillar, which was designed to hold the saint's mortal remains. They thus define the space of the large church, erecting an original circular plan with three naves placed one behind the other.

In order to build these futuristic arches – the average span of the inner arches is 131 ft (40 m) – Renzo Piano defied the laws of statics. On the one hand he chose to use stone, a traditional material typically used for sacred architecture; but on the other, he used it to implement an avant-garde technology so as to increase its technical performance to the maximum. Each arch is in fact made of a series of pre-fabricated quoins made from Apricena stone. They were designed using sophisticated software, and pre-compressed using an inner reinforcement of steel cables; this gave them adequate resistance to traction in the event of orthogonal stress to the plane of the arch, as happens during earthquakes, for example. Again, to guarantee the utmost efficiency of the structure under stress, the quoins were assembled in blocks of 5-6 pieces to form maxi-quoins; a layer of fiber-reinforced cement

210 ■ In the foreground of the main liturgical entrance are the baptismal font and the bronze doors by artist Mimmo Paladino, which are inserted into the copper sheets.

containing stainless steel metal fibers was inserted between each pair, able to disperse the energy produced by any seismic activity.

The 17 large arches support the laminated wood structure of the roof through 165 triangular stainless steel struts attached to steel plates placed between the maxi-quoins. The relative slenderness of these elements creates an effect of lightness as though the roof were suspended in the air. This is accentuated by the jumps in height of the various sloped surfaces which make up the roof itself, which natural light filters through. A light-well lets light directly onto the stone altar and onto the suspended gilt bronze cross, by the artist Arnaldo Pomodoro.

211 top ■ The inner space of the sanctuary is remarkable for its large parabolic arches. In the background is the stained glass window, with 84 panels of the Apocalypse, taken from a series of tapestries from the Angers cycle.

211 bottom ■ This photograph shows the large outside wall of the parvis, with its sequence of bells and the large cross, 131.2 ft (40 m) high.

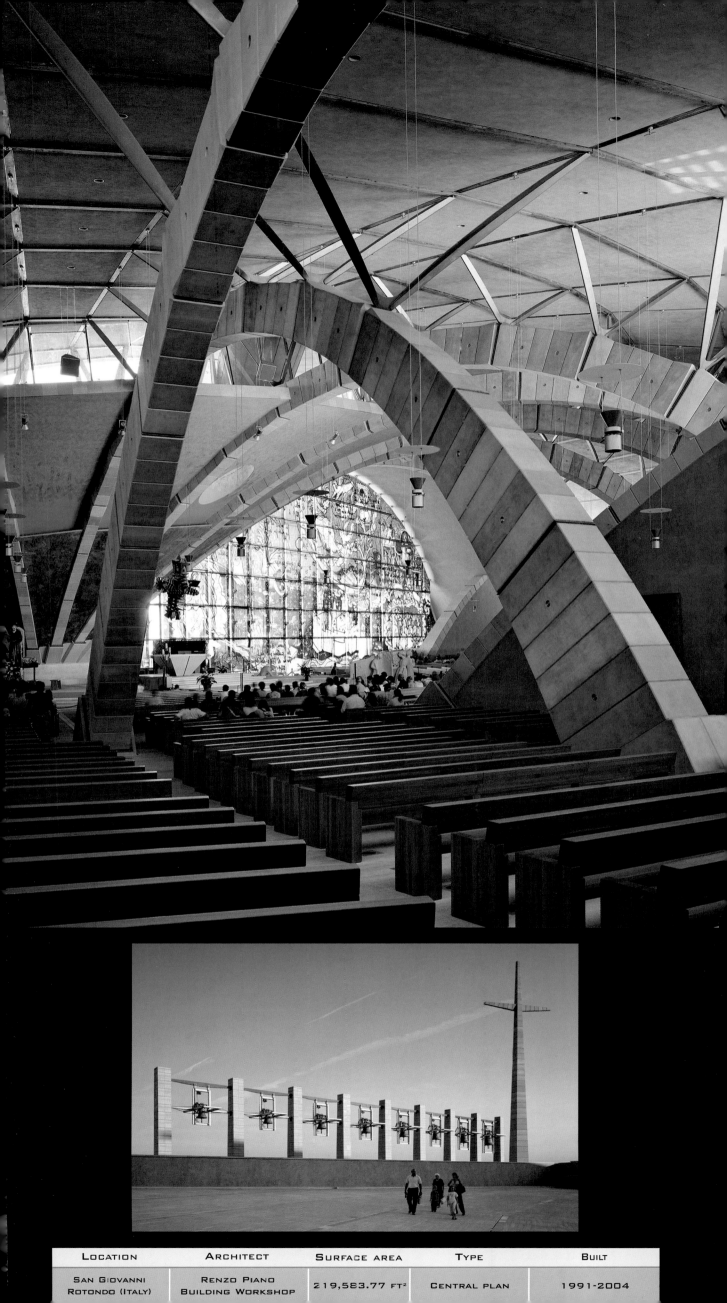

LOCATION	ARCHITECT	SURFACE AREA	TYPE	BUILT
SAN GIOVANNI ROTONDO (ITALY)	RENZO PIANO BUILDING WORKSHOP	219,583.77 FT²	CENTRAL PLAN	1991-2004

essential bibliography

Richard Krautheimer, *Architettura paleocristiana e bizantina*, Einaudi, Turin 1986

Rolf Toman, *Romanesque: Architecture, Sculpture, Painting*, (Könemann, originally published Cologne 1996)

Anne Prache, *La cattedrale dalle origini al gotico*, Jaca Book, Milan 1999

Willibald Sauerländer, *La cattedrale gotica: 1140-1260*, Rizzoli, Milan 1991

Christopher Wilson, *The gothic cathedral: the architecture of the great church 1130-1530*, Thames and Hudson, London 1990

Arturo Carlo Quintavalle, *Il medioevo delle cattedrali*, Skira, Milan 2006

Bernhard Schütz, *Great cathedrals*, Harry N. Abrams, New York 2002

Leonardo Benevolo, *Storia dell'architettura del Rinascimento*, Laterza, Rome-Bari 2002 (new edition)

Manfredo Tafuri, *Ricerca del Rinascimento: principi, città, architetti*, Einaudi, Turin 1992

Bruno Adorni (editor), *La chiesa a pianta centrale: tempio civico del Rinascimento*, Electa, Milan 2002

Cesare de Seta, *Architetture della fede in Italia*, Mondadori, Milan 2003

Gianni Mezzanotte, *Giovanni Muzio: architetture francescane*, Eris, Milan 1974

Maria Maddalena Torricella, *Gio Ponti 1964-1971. Progetto e costruzione di una cattedrale. La Gran Madre di Dio a Taranto*, Edizioni Pugliesi, Martina Franca 2004

Various authors: *Mario Botta. La cattedrale di Evry*, Skira, Milan 1996

Renzo Piano Building Workshop, *La chiesa di Padre Pio a San Giovanni Rotondo*, Motta, Milan 2005

index

c = caption   boldface = specific chapter

index

index

photographic references

A. H. Acland/Architectural Association: pages 102-103
AISA: pages 15 (seventh foto), 67 (second, third and fourth photo), 76, 80-81, 82, 85, 99, 100 bottom, 117 (fifth foto), 136-137, 162
Alamy Images: page 15 (fourth photo)
Bernard Annebique/Corbis Sygma/Corbis: page 71 left
Archivio Alinari: pages 128-129, 129 top
Archivio Iconografico, S.A./Corbis: pages 15 (first photo), 90-91, 146, 183 (second photo)
Archivio Muzio - Milano: pages 186 top and bottom
Archivio Scala: pages 20, 20-21, 21, 44, 46 top and bottom, 52 bottom left and right, 65 top, 67 (first and seeventh photo), 73, 112, 114-115, 121 bottom left and right, 124-125, 183 (fifth photo)
Jura Artamonov: pages 150 top and bottom, 152 top and bottom, 153
Artedia: page 183 (eighth photo)
Yann Arthus-Bertrand/Corbis: pages 70-71
Antonio Attini/Archivio White Star: pages 16-17, 17 top and bottom, 18, 18-19, 19 top and bottom, 48-49, 108, 110-111, 126, 187 left and right
Wilfried Bahnmüller: page 107
Guido Baviera: page 123 bottom
Marcello Bertinetti/Archivio White Star: pages 32 top, 33, 38, 39, 49 left and right, 117 (third photo), 149
Michèle Bellot/Photo RMN: page 117 (eighth photo)
Bibliothèque nationale de France: page 79 bottom
Gérard Blot/Photo RMN: page 63
Bridgeman/Archivio Alinari: pages 42, 156 bottom left and right

Federico Brunetti: page 183 (sixth photo)
Richard Bryant/arcaid.co.uk: page 183 (nineth photo)
Wojtek Buss/Agefotostock/Contrasto: page 170
Cameraphoto: pages 10-11, 31, 34, 35, 36 top, center and bottom
Elio and Stefano Ciol: page 109
Angelo Colombo/Archivio White Star: pages 22, 118, 132, 144 top, 166, 175 bottom
Guido Cozzi/Atlantide Photo Travel: page 124
Giovanni Dagli Orti/The Art Archive: pages 50, 147
Giuseppe Dall'Arche/Sime/Sie: page 47
Enrique del Rivero: pages 98, 101
Michel Denancé/Artedia: pages 192-193, 210, 211 top and bottom
Jay Dickman/Corbis: page 173
Didier Dorval/Masterfile/Sie: page 125
Patrick Durand/Corbis Sygma/Corbis: page 70
Durham University Library: page 56 top
Editions Gaud: pages 64, 65 bottom left and right
Macduff Everton/Corbis: page 165 bottom
Fabbrica di San Pietro in Vaticano: page 135
Peter Ferstl: page 104
Fototeca del Centro Internazionale di Studi di Architettura Andrea Palladio: pages 138, 139 bottom left and right
Franz-Marc Frei/Corbis: pages 92-93
Patrick Frilet/Hemispheres Images: page 183 (first photo)
Bertrand Gardel/Hemispheres Images: pages 62-63

Tony Gentile/Reuters/Contrasto: page 209 top
Cesare Gerolimetto/Archivio White Star: pages 186-187
Scott Gilchrist/Archivision: pages 41, 72, 81 top, 113, 122, 123 top, 133, 159 top and bottom, 171, 191
Gunter Grafenhain/Sime/Sie: pages 150-151
Itamar Grinberg/Archivio White Star: pages 184-185
Paul Hardy/Corbis: pages 30-31
Jason Hawkes/Corbis: pages 55, 88-89, 117 (seventh photo)
Heinz Hebeisen/Iberimage: pages 143 bottom, 145, 163
Robert Holmes/Corbis: page 117 (sixth photo)
Angelo Hornak/Corbis: pages 56 bottom, 57, 60 center, 67 (fifth photo), 87 top, 91 left, 93, 96
Angelo Hornak Photo Library: page 88
Angelo Hornak Photo Library, courtesy of the Dean and Chapter, Canterbury: page 90
Angelo Hornak Photo Library, courtesy of the Dean and Chapter, Wells: page 97
Angelo Hornak Photo Library, courtesy of Westminster Cathedral: page 180
Colin Hoskins; Cordaiy Photo Library Ltd./Corbis: page 95
Johanna Huber/Sime/Sie: pages 5, 15 (third photo), 134-135
Shunji Ishida/RPBW: pages 208-209
Jarrold Publishing: page 181 top
Christian Jean/Photo RMN: pages 83, 110
Peter Jeffree/Architectural Association: page 179
KPA/Picture-alliance: page 105

photographic references

Philip Keirle/Architectural Association: page 94

Waltraud Klammet: pages 44-45

Javier Larrea/AgeFotostock/Marka: pages 146-147

Erich Lessing/Contrasto: pages 15 (fifth photo), 28 top, center and bottom, 29, 37, 52 top, 53, 60 top, 67 (sixth photo), 91 right, 117 (fourth photo), 127, 129 bottom, 140, 141 top, 169

Hervé Lewandowski/Photo RMN: page 111

Diego Lezama Orezzoli/Corbis: pages 172, 188-189, 190-191

Liao Yusheng: pages 194-195, 195 top and bottom

Marcello Libra/Archivio White Star: page 106

Massimo Listri/Corbis: page 117 (first photo)

Sampson Lloyd: page 154

London Aerial Photo Library/Corbis: pages 155, 178

Marka Collection: page 15 (eighth photo)

Paolo Marton: page 139 top

Florian Monheim/www.bildarchiv-monheim.de: page 77

Osamu Murai: page 192

Opera Primaziale Pisana - Franco Cosimo Panini Editore: page 43

Oronoz/Photo12.com: page 100 top

Arturo Osorno: page 164

Richard Payne: pages 200, 201, 202-203

Photoservice Electa/Akg: pages 12-13, 15 (sixth photo), 48, 50-51, 84, 87 bottom, 143 top, 144 bottom, 167, 168, 183 (fourth photo)

Renzo Piano Building Workshop: page 209 bottom

Picture-alliance: page 141 bottom

Paul Raftery/View Pictures: page 183 (third photo)

Luciano Ramires/Archivio White Star: pages 59, 61

Bertrand Riege/Hemispheres Images: pages 26-27

Massimo Ripani/Sime/Sie: pages 69, 71 right

Ghigo Roli/Eikonos: pages 196, 197

Nicolas Sapieha/The Art Archive: page 165 top

Dae Sasitorn/lastrefuge.co.uk: page 157

Giovanni Simeone/Sime/Sie: pages 74-75, 130-131, 131

Mark Smith: page 40 bottom left

Stahli/AgeFotostock/Marka: page 183 (seventh photo)

Studio Architetto Mario Botta/Mario Botta: page 207

Studio Architetto Mario Botta/Pino Musi: pages 204, 206 bottom, 206-207

SuperStock/AgeFotostock/Marka: page 205

Nicolas Tavernier/Rea/Contrasto: page 206 top

Agostino Temporelli, Mauro Gavinelli, Vincenzo Mirarchi/Agenzia HAL9000 S.r.l. - Novara: page 174

TopFoto/ICP: pages 156 top, 160-161

Ruggero Vanni/Corbis: pages 86-87

Sandro Vannini/Corbis: pages 7, 78-79, 79 left, 81 bottom, 117 (second photo)

Giulio Veggi/Archivio White Star: pages 15 (second photo), 22-23, 40 top, 40 bottom right, 121 top, 149, 158, 181 bottom

Adam Woolfitt/Corbis: pages 24-25, 58

Pawel Wysocki/Hemispheres Images: page 24

Michael S. Yamashita/Corbis: page 119

Jim Zuckerman/Corbis: pages 120-121

Courtesy of the Archivio Arcivescovo Motolese, Taranto: pages 198 top and bottom, 199

Courtesy of the Archivio di Stato di Novara: pages 175 top, 176

Courtesy of the Canonico Archivista della Basilica di San Gaudenzio, don Agostino Temporelli: pages 176-177

Courtesy of the Musée de Nôtre-Dame de Paris: page 68

Courtesy of the Procuratoria di San Marco, Venezia: page 32 bottom

Acknowledgments

The author would like to thank:

Maria Teresa Feraboli for having written the texts on the churches in Germany, the United Kingdom, Russia and on Crystal Cathedral (United States)

Fulvio Irace, Don Romeo Cavedo, Roberto Mazzetti, Baran and Rosy Ciagà

The publisher would like to thank:

Province of Novara Local Tourism Board, in particular Paola Colombo

Archivio Arcivescovo Motolese, Taranto, in particular Vittorio De Marco

Novara State Archive, in particular the Director Maria Marcella Vallascas

Muzio Archive, Milan, in particular Giovanni Muzio

Archdiocese of Taranto, in particular the Cultural Heritage Manager Don Giuseppe Russo

Canterbury Cathedral Archives, in particular Cressida Annesley and Angela Prior

Centro Internazionale di Studi di Architettura Andrea Palladio, Vicenza, in particular Elisabetta Michelato

Curia Diocesana di Novara, in particular the Canonical Archiveist of the basilica of San Gaudenzio, Don Agostino Temporelli

Durham University Library, Archives and Special Collections, in particular Richard Higgins

Fundação Oscar Niemeyer, Rio de Janeiro, in particular Fernanda Martins

Gabinetto dei Disegni e delle Stampe degli Uffizi, Florence, in particular Elisabetta Bandinelli Fossi

Gio Ponti Archives, in particular Salvatore Licitra

Kenzo Tange Associates, Tokyo, in particular Denise Tange

Anna Leone, Moscow

Musée de Nôtre-Dame de Paris, in particular the Curator Anne-Marie Joly

Opera della Primaziale Pisana, in particular Diego Guidi

Burgos Province Tourist Board, in particular Raquel Puente

Philip Johnson - Alan Ritchie Architects, New York, in particular Alan Ritchie

Procuratoria di San Marco, Venice, in particular Paolo Gasparotto

Renzo Piano Building Workshop, in particular Stefania Canta and Chiara Casazza

St Paul's Cathedral Press Office, in particular Lorna Fletcher

Studio Architetto Mario Botta, in particular Elisiana Di Bernardo

Tutela e Conservazione Beni Culturali della Fabbrica di San Pietro, Città del Vaticano, in particular Pietro Zander

Westminster Cathedral Editorial Office, in particular Susan Claridge and Blandine Tugendhat